Southern Literary Studies
Louis D. Rubin, Jr., Editor

John Crowe Ransom's Secular Faith

John Crowe Ransom's Secular Faith

Kieran Quinlan

LOUISIANA STATE UNIVERSITY PRESS
Baton Rouge and London

98 97 96 95 94 93 92 91 90 89   5 4 3 2 1

Designer: Sylvia Malik Loftin
Typeface: Palatino
Typesetter: G&S Typesetters, Inc.
Printer: Thomson-Shore, Inc.
Binder: John H. Dekker & Sons, Inc.

Library of Congress Cataloging-in-Publication Data

Quinlan, Kieran, 1945–
    John Crowe Ransom's secular faith/Kieran Quinlan.
        p.   cm.—(Southern literary studies)
    Bibliography: p.
    Includes index.
    ISBN 0-8071-1471-5
        1. Ransom, John Crowe, 1888–1974—Philosophy.   2. Belief and doubt
in literature.   3. Philosophy in literature.   I. Title.
II. Series.
PS3535.A635Z83   1989   88-7850
811'.52—dc19   CIP

Grateful acknowledgment is made to Helen Ransom Forman for permission to quote extensively from John Crowe Ransom's writings; to
Robert Penn Warren for permission to quote from his May 5, 1985,
letter to the author; to Alfred A. Knopf, Inc., for permission to use
excerpts from Wallace Stevens' poem "Adagia," copyright 1957, in
Opus Posthumous, and "Sunday Morning," copyright 1923, in The Collected Poems of Wallace Stevens; and to the Kenyon College Archives for
permission to use excerpts from the November 1, 1974, program for
Ransom's memorial service. Portions of this book that deal with the
relationship between Ransom and T. S. Eliot appeared in somewhat
different form in "Sacred Eliot, Secular Ransom: Dead Opposites,"
Kenyon Review, n.s., X, No. 4 (Fall, 1988). Copyright by Kenyon
College.

The paper in this book meets the guidelines for permanence and dura-
bility of the Committee on Production Guidelines for Book Longevity
of the Council on Library Resources. ∞

For TDY

The presence of God within the object, as it existed for the early romantics, is forgotten, and forgotten is the pathos of the Victorians' reaching out for a God disappearing over the horizon of an objectified world. . . . Many people have forgotten that they have forgotten the death of God, the living God of Abraham and Isaac, Dante and Pascal. Many who believe that they believe in God believe in him only as the highest value, that is, as a creation of man, the inventor of values.

—J. Hillis Miller, *Poets of Reality*

The final belief is to believe in a fiction, which you know to be a fiction, there being nothing else.

—Wallace Stevens, *Adagia*

There is one poet whose universals seem to be lost on our critics, though directed specifically to our age and important to it. . . . [S]o far as I have read them none has said anything even remotely to this effect: that the poems of [Wallace] Stevens from the first volume onward may be construed as a set of Notes Toward the Definition of a Secular Culture, and would therefore stand in some opposition to T. S. Eliot's Notes Toward the Definition of Culture as Based on Religion, with which we have been made acquainted both in verse and in prose.

—John Crowe Ransom, "The Concrete Universal, I"

Contents

Preface

The publication in recent years of several important books and articles by and about John Crowe Ransom—most notably Thomas Daniel Young's biography in 1976, the *Selected Essays of John Crowe Ransom* in 1984, and the *Selected Letters of John Crowe Ransom* since then—has highlighted a number of apparent discrepancies in this writer's life and thought that suggest, not only that there is still some question as to the intention and shape of his literary and intellectual career, but that, in addition, looking for an answer to the problem is of more than simply academic interest.[1] Hence arises the need for the present study.

The discontinuities in Ransom's life are by now fairly obvious: a successful poet, he spent the greater part of his career in the composition of prose; a southern agrarian in the 1930s, he later rejected the movement as nostalgic and unrealistic; a political conservative, he became a staunch New Dealer, even admitting on one occasion that Marxism was the only generous ideology still remaining; a mentor for the New Critics with their "exclusive" attention to the text itself, he subsequently called for the use of psychology, sociology, and anthropology in the conduct of literary studies; a vigorous opponent of contemporary positivistic philosophy, he gradually came to agree with many of its perplexing conclusions; and, most importantly, the descendant of Methodist ministers and the author of a famous defense of religion, he believed neither in

---

1. Thomas Daniel Young, *Gentleman in a Dustcoat: A Biography of John Crowe Ransom* (Baton Rouge, 1976); Thomas Daniel Young and John Hindle (eds.), *Selected Essays of John Crowe Ransom* (Baton Rouge, 1984); Thomas Daniel Young and George Core (eds.), *Selected Letters of John Crowe Ransom* (Baton Rouge, 1985). *Selected Essays* and *Selected Letters* will hereinafter be cited parenthetically by page number throughout the text as *SE* and *SL*, respectively.

the concept of religious revelation, nor in the divinity of Christ, and least of all in the promise of an afterlife. Even as early as 1969, Monroe K. Spears noted that "Ransom himself has always remained a thoroughgoing skeptic: beneath the personal charm and the gentle and courteous manner he has been detached, unbelieving, unillusioned, perhaps inclining rather more to the scientific attitude, or at least increasingly sympathetic toward it. There has been a radical, hard-headed skepticism, a kind of bleakness, beneath the 'traditional' surface."[2] In short, then, Ransom was not always quite what he seemed to be.

Still, though attention is increasingly being paid to these apparent discontinuities in Ransom's thought—in recent essays by Louis D. Rubin, Michael O'Brien, Richard H. King, Daniel Joseph Singal, Geoffrey Hill, and Albert Gelpi, for example—so far there has been little attempt to offer an explanation for them within the context of the poet's entire career.[3] It might even be claimed that the prevailing view continues to be that Ransom was a defender of the more conservative religious and aesthetic orthodoxies of his day, albeit now seen as deeply troubled and inconsistent in his intellectual maneuvering. In the latest volume of *A History of Modern Criticism, 1750–1950*, René Wellek provides a typical example of such a judgment: "The religious implications and motives [of Ransom's writings] are obvious in the late passages as they are in the early book *God Without Thunder*. [But] I would not want to decide how they can be reconciled with the strong naturalistic statements quoted before, with the view that poets are 'prodigious materialists.' . . . Transcendence seems expressly denied in these pronouncements."[4]

2. Monroe K. Spears, *Dionysus and the City: Modernism in Twentieth-Century Poetry* (New York, 1970), 158–59.
3. Louis D. Rubin, *The Wary Fugitives: Four Poets and the South* (Baton Rouge, 1978); Michael O'Brien, *The Idea of the American South, 1920–1941* (Baltimore, 1979); Richard H. King, *A Southern Renaissance: The Cultural Awakening of the American South, 1930–1955* (New York, 1981); Daniel Joseph Singal, *The War Within: From Victorian to Modernist Thought in the South, 1919–1945* (Chapel Hill, 1982); Geoffrey Hill, *The Lords of Limit: Essays on Literature and Ideas* (New York, 1984); Albert Gelpi, *A Coherent Splendor: The American Poetic Renaissance, 1910–1950* (New York, 1987). Although he barely touches on Ransom's poetry as such, in *The Critical Twilight: Explorations in the Ideology of Anglo-American Literary Theory from Eliot to McLuhan* (London, 1977), 41–103, John Fekete offers quite a detailed account of the main stages of Ransom's progress as seen from a Marxist perspective.
4. René Wellek, *American Criticism, 1900–1950* (New Haven, 1986), 165–66, Vol. VI of Wellek, *A History of Modern Criticism, 1750–1950*.

It is, then, precisely to this kind of problem that the present study addresses itself in the hope of providing a satisfactory solution. My argument is that the key to Ransom's development lies in his early rejection of the tenets of Christian theology and in his consequent effort to articulate an alternative philosophy to live by. Indeed, Ransom always considered himself to be as much a philosopher—and not wholly an amateur one—as a poet and critic. Furthermore, in what was to be the last of a lifelong series of observations on T. S. Eliot's progress, he noted that the attempt to recover a lost religious faith is "the point of the argument" of all of his fellow American's poetry.[5] The attempt to come to terms with the consequences of an early loss of belief is also the determining argument of Ransom's own texts, but they are texts in which he states over and over again his preference for the tangible reality of a world validated by an empiricist rather than a transcendentalist philosophy.

What follows, therefore, is offered as a new interpretation of this writer's life and work. And yet, I would want to argue that it has more authority than that. The author of "A Poem Nearly Anonymous" (a 1933 essay on Milton's *Lycidas*) is still mistakenly seen as impersonal and secretive in expressing his views on important matters when, in truth, he has staked out very clearly almost every step of his intellectual and emotional journey. Denis Donoghue is quite correct when he observes that Ransom is always "talking to himself, to begin with," and this circumstance accounts for what in his essays often appears to be a wandering from the topic in hand or the making of an aside that seems irrelevant to the main argument.[6] But, in the end, the privacy is more apparent than real, and, indeed, in *The Wary Fugitives*, Louis D. Rubin has shown in considerable detail how Ransom's comments on Milton even in the essay just mentioned have little exact reference to the historical English poet and are instead "Ransom on Ransom," Milton functioning largely as a cipher for the problems that were preoccupying Ransom at the time.[7] From the days of the Hardyesque *Poems About*

5. John Crowe Ransom, *The World's Body* (Baton Rouge, 1968), 353, hereinafter cited parenthetically throughout the text as *WB*.
6. Denis Donoghue, *Ferocious Alphabets* (Boston, 1981), 52.
7. Rubin, *The Wary Fugitives*, 282. Rubin goes so far as to suggest that Ransom's claim in "A Poem Nearly Anonymous" (*WB*, 1–28) that Milton had abandoned "that career in the church which his father had intended for him and to which he seems at first to have consented" might well have applied to "this son and grandson of Meth-

God in 1919, through the period of the agnostic "Necrological,"
"Bells for John Whiteside's Daughter," and other such poems (those
for which he is largely remembered), and especially in the essays of
the early 1940s that show him reluctantly coming to sympathize
with the antimetaphysical naturalist and logical-positivist philosophers and sharply critical of the religious views of T. S. Eliot and
Allen Tate, Ransom is always turning aside to offer a personal comment or to make yet another declaration of his own "faith." Tate
himself has even gently criticized that urgent logic within his
friend that led Ransom continually—and often against the advice
of his associates—to make public repudiation of his previous position every time he altered his opinion on a particular issue.

Ransom's is, for the most part, a well-documented journey in unbelief in which he identifies quite explicitly with the secular faith of
Wallace Stevens' "Sunday Morning" as against the Christian affirmation of Eliot's major poems. If the appeal of Eliot's religious
search lies in his unique encounter with personal despair and his
eventual triumph over it, perhaps the appeal of Ransom's is to be
found in his discerning examination of the arguments that might
present themselves to any philosophically minded seeker for an
answer to the riddle of mortality and in the poet's willingness
to accept the sobering consequences of his findings. Certainly
Ransom is not a professional philosopher by the standards that
have tended to prevail in academic circles in recent decades, but he
is nonetheless engaged with the issue of belief and its validity at
the level at which many intelligent persons still make their fundamental decisions; he belongs firmly to that tradition of culture
criticism that Richard Rorty has been commending recently as necessary for the functioning of our society, though it may not offer any metaphysical comfort in an idealistic sense: "In such a culture, Jonathan Edwards and Thomas Jefferson, Henry and William
James, John Dewey and Thorstein Veblen will all be present. No
one will be asking . . . perhaps, which ones are the philosophers."[8]

---

odist ministers" himself (283). I. A. Richards and Donald Davie, among several
others, have made similar criticisms in regard to various commentaries by Ransom.
Later in his career, Ransom was frequently to use a phrase in his own regard in one
essay and then apply it to Hardy, Stevens, or Eliot in another without any indication
of its origin. Although an excellent and sympathetic editor, Ransom was also a
"strong" misreader of those texts that particularly interested him.

8. Richard Rorty, "Genteel Syntheses, Professional Analyses, Transcendentalist Culture," in Peter Caws (ed.), *Two Centuries of Philosophy in America* (Totowa,
N.J., 1980), 239.

Finally, it is important to keep in mind that, as George Core and others have argued, Ransom's "was not a life merely literary" (*SL*, 14). But what was not literary about it—its domestic side, for example, his warm friendships, his enormous enthusiasm for games and sports of all kinds—has, with few exceptions, entered into his poetry and prose even less so than that of such a reclusive couple as Wallace and Elsie Stevens. Yet, though the details of such concerns do not form part of my narrative, they are its essential backdrop: Ransom did indeed very actively engage in loving those "precious objects" of "the world's body" that he so frequently commended to others. His granddaughter, novelist Robb Forman Dew, conveys the spirit of one important aspect of what I am referring to in her essay "Summer's End": "I can't imagine how it must have been for my grandmother to have been married to a man moderately well known in his lifetime. I think that when they were first married, at least in her circles, it was she who was celebrated, being a beauty and having married a professor of no particular social standing. She was a competitive woman, and so, surely, all the attention paid him must have sometimes been abrasive to her, but they seemed to love each other, and I think they had a real romance."[9] Although Ransom's personal celebration of worldly love, and variety, and beauty may not have been a totally adequate response to a universe in which also "ignorant armies clash by night," he—more hopefully than Arnold—thought of it, rightly or wrongly, as truly the best response available in the present circumstances.

9. Robb Forman Dew, "Summer's End," *Mississippi Quarterly*, XXX (Winter, 1976–77), 145.

Acknowledgments

Robert Penn Warren, in spite of poor eyesight, read a synopsis of my original manuscript in essay form and offered additional commentary. At Vanderbilt University, Donald Davie provided cautionary observations from time to time; William T. Bandy was always willing to pause from his labors on Baudelaire to discuss his old teacher; and Marice Wolfe facilitated use of the Ransom materials in the Special Collections of the Jean and Alexander Heard Library. At Kenyon College, Thomas B. Greenslade answered some rather unusual questions concerning the poet's burial services there. At the University of California, Irvine, during the earthshaking summer of 1986, John Carlos Rowe (under the sponsorship of the National Endowment for the Humanities) attempted to sharpen my awareness of the contemporary debate in critical theory. Beverly Jarrett, Catherine Barton, Catherine Silvia, and especially Catherine Landry of Louisiana State University Press made completion of the project as pleasant as possible in the circumstances. First and last, of course, I am grateful to Thomas Daniel Young, who, even when he had reservations about what I wanted to say, always encouraged me to say it. To all of these, and to John Adams, Tom Brown, and Flowers Braswell, my sincerest thanks.

John Crowe Ransom's Secular Faith

1

Religious Backsliding

Throughout the winter of 1942–1943, when Robert Lowell was in his most combative Catholic phase and quite a nuisance to all who came in contact with him, he was engaged in what his biographer refers to as a "stern domestic regimen" of religious activities, crowned by his insistence that his wife Jean Stafford remarry him in the Roman church because he now considered that their marriage prior to his conversion had been "invalid." The poems that he was writing—those that would later make up *Land of Unlikeness* and *Winter Sea*—were "cries for us to recover our ancient freedom and dignity, to be Christian and build a Christian society." Lowell submitted several of these to John Crowe Ransom for the *Kenyon Review*, accompanied by a short prose essay in defense of religious belief. The sequel is especially instructive, not only in that here there was a confrontation between two radically different, though equally stubborn, temperaments who yet held each other in the highest esteem—Lowell always regarded Ransom as his most important mentor, while Ransom had recommended the young poet to Cleanth Brooks and Robert Penn Warren as "more than a student, he's more like a son to me"—but that the confrontation came at a time when their respective intellectual commitments were farther apart than they had ever been before or probably would be again in the future.[1]

While Lowell had lately turned to neo-Thomism under the influence of reading Étienne Gilson and Jacques Maritain, among others, Ransom had been moving in totally the opposite direction. This was partly because of his distaste for the fuzziness of Maritain's writings (which he had nevertheless published in the *Kenyon Re-*

1. Ian Hamilton, *Robert Lowell: A Biography* (New York, 1982), 79, 83, 72.

view), but more so on account of his increasing sympathy with certain aspects of the logical-positivist movement with which he was becoming directly acquainted during this period. Whereas a few years earlier he had tended to defend religion—albeit of a very unorthodox variety defended with equally unorthodox arguments—against its various detractors, now he was vigorously attacking Eliot and Tate in particular for what he perceived as their benighted attitudes. Hence his letter to Lowell on April 27, 1943, accepting some of the poems also makes very clear his rejection of Lowell's religious viewpoint:

> I'll give my objection to your position very briefly without documenting it. I think you argue that Thomism makes for human happiness, and I'm aware that it does, with *many minds;* with others it doesn't work. Thomism is philosophy as well as recorded "revelation"; as philosophy it's exposed to the liabilities of philosophy, and is countered by other philosophy. You are too easy about that, saying that "by guaranteeing certain demonstrable but arduous truths, Christian Revelation did actually confirm and liberate philosophy." But how can somebody else (was it the Pope, about 1870?) guarantee a truth to us? In what manner will compensation be made if it's found to be falsity rather than truth? And what were the specific arduous truths? You tend to want a kind of philosophy that subordinates itself, and quits applying its method, at a certain point; but that's not philosophy in my estimation.   (*SL,* 308)

Lowell would subsequently abandon Catholicism with its Thomistic intellectualizing, not because of what Ransom had written, but rather because, as Stafford unkindly commented, "it had served its *literary* purpose"; perhaps in this light it might be said that Ransom had abandoned poetry in 1927 because it had served its *philosophical* purpose. At all events, what is important about the letter is that it shows just how deeply Ransom was committed to the requirements of a thoroughly philosophical investigation of the grounds of human activities and beliefs. He was to state the matter even more forcefully some years later in criticizing Maritain for attempting "to keep alive the tangle of Thomist thought after six centuries" when what was needed was "a better anthropology, a better psychology to define this [religious] kind of experience," rather than a more "ingenious metaphysics." Ransom's judgment was that "there is no hope of understanding religion unless it can receive a modern and therefore secular description."[2] Meanwhile,

2. *Ibid.,* 121; John Crowe Ransom, Review of Jacques Maritain's *The Dream of Descartes,* in *Sewanee Review,* LIV (Winter, 1946), 156.

he himself was continually attempting to define such a secular faith in a manner that would have some kind of philosophical validity. It was only, however, after Ransom had suffered his own loss of belief in the tradition into which he had been born in 1888 in rural Tennessee that he began this process of redefining the religious experience: his starting point, like that of many other writers of the twentieth century, had been with the great Victorian doubters, and in his case with Matthew Arnold and Thomas Hardy in particular.

Ransom had "backslid" (to use his own expression) from his father's faith sometime before going to Oxford in 1910 at the age of twenty-two (WB, 376). Growing up in the household of quite a well-educated clergyman, where the religious controversies of the day were talked about in a surprisingly open manner (his mother frequently worried that the animated discussions between father and son might lead the neighbors to think that they were quarreling), he was early exposed to the higher criticism of the Bible that had developed extensively in the German universities in the nineteenth century and that had troubled the faith of many thoughtful believers in England after its widespread dissemination there in 1860 with the publication of *Essays and Reviews*. These new theories concerning such matters as the authorship of the Pentateuch and the Book of Isaiah, the historical accuracy of the events of the Old Testament, and the dating of the various gospel accounts of the life of Jesus, became controversial a few decades later in America, where they were heatedly debated within the denominations themselves and popularized in the various church periodicals: the editor of the *Methodist Quarterly Review*, for example, an associate of Ransom's father, was severely criticized for printing so many articles on such controversial topics. Since this reevaluation of the biblical text questioned in particular the validity of the supernatural events recorded there and, in general, felt pressed to offer a more naturalistic explanation for them in order to preserve a liberal and intelligent faith in a new scientific age, the result was that Ransom's confidence in the historical truth of the Bible was shaken in much the same way that Matthew Arnold's had been. On several occasions in later years, Ransom was to draw attention to the parallel between his own experience and that of the English writer: "To me the most resonant and tragic version of the decline of institutional religion has been Arnold's perfect statement, pointing to the

vulnerable spot in the defense of the establishment by its guard-
ians: 'Our religion has materialized itself in the fact, in the supposed fact; it has attached its emotion to the fact, and now the fact
is failing it.' The Old Testament they regarded as history, till upset
by their own 'liberal theologians' a short while ago; and the dam-
age spread, much more than inferentially, to the reputation of the
New Testament."[3]

By the time he made that remark—1941—Ransom had distanced
himself so far from professing any religious orthodoxy whatsoever
that the believers in all such creedal systems had become a mere
"they." Still, while he was never really to elaborate on any of its
details or to mention—apart from a single reference to the liberal
German theologian Schleiermacher—the sources he had read, this
criticism of the Bible that he had encountered as a youth always
remained the cornerstone of his subsequent religious disbelief and
of his distrust of any kind of supernaturalism. When he was a
young English instructor at Vanderbilt University in Nashville after
World War I, his favorite topic of discussion with his students
in his college rooms is reported to have been "the extent to which
the higher criticism of the Bible had undermined the elements of
Christian faith."[4] Furthermore, here also lay the remote origins of
Ransom's interest in literary theory: it was precisely because the
traditional creeds had been shaken by the scrutiny of textual and
historical criticism that they would have to survive—as Arnold had
clearly indicated—as poetry, faithful to the truth of the human
imagination rather than to the uncertainties of factual discoveries.[5]

3. Ferenc Morton Szasz, *The Divided Mind of Protestant America, 1880–1930* (University, Ala., 1982), 39–40; John Crowe Ransom, *The New Criticism* (New York, 1941),
202–203, hereinafter cited parenthetically by page number in the text, as *NC* where
necessary for clarity.

4. Young, *Gentleman in a Dustcoat*, 91.

5. Ruth apRoberts' remarks on Arnold's progress from religion to a theory of
religion and to aesthetics are relevant also to Ransom's intellectual development:
Arnold "consistently questions convention in theology and in criticism, holding experience as the sole validity. . . . It is Arnold's refusal to systematize, to dogmatize,
that makes for the splendidly British-empirical loose ends in his argument, grand
inconsistencies that leave room for modern aesthetics. It is hardly to be expected of
him that he should exploit his discovery in theory and proceed to invent William
James, Susanne Langer, Wittgenstein, Logical Positivism, Vaihinger, Stevens, and
the Supreme Fiction. But it is from data like Arnold's, and from attitudes like his,
that all these have developed. And perhaps none of these has been so securely
based as he in a broad experience of literature, secular and religious" (*Arnold and
God* [Berkeley, 1983], 228–29).

Ransom's judgment on the matter, however, was made quite independently and over a period of time: Arnold's experience offered a parallel, not a model. Ransom's loss was his own, and his father, for instance, like many another liberal minister of the Methodist church, does not appear to have been unduly disturbed by the new theories. Whether this loss was accompanied by emotional distress is a question that is likely to remain unanswered as there is little detailed record of Ransom's progress at the time. Years later, in a review of E. D. H. Johnson's *The Alien Vision of Victorian Poetry*, Ransom would simply refer to Arnold as suffering "from the breakdown of faith, which perhaps was the most poignant of the spiritual maladies of the Century"; "if our Century seems different," he continues, "it may be because an acute pain has become chronic and low-grade, so that perhaps most writers just make the best of it."[6]

While the relativizing of the Christian faith that the higher criticism left in its wake certainly cast doubt on the unique promises made by the churches to their followers, it did not in itself disprove the existence of some kind of deity, or even the experiential basis on which the religious superstructure had been built. Schleiermacher, for example, had argued for the religious experience as the "most highly and fully developed form of self-consciousness."[7] Nevertheless, it was now possible—and in a way necessary—to rethink the previously accepted questions and answers as to the ultimate nature of reality, for it might be that whatever deity existed was quite other than had traditionally been envisaged; at the very least, the Christian paradigm of a Creator who was good, had been rebelled against, but had finally forgiven sinful mankind was no longer the only one conceivable.

Ransom's initial response to the crisis appears to have been along Manichean lines: if a divine power existed, it must contain within itself whatever good and evil were to be found in the real world. Although in arriving at this tentative conclusion he was probably influenced by his undergraduate study of Thomas Hardy—whom he also thought had been disturbed by Darwin's theories and the higher criticism of the Bible—once again, the English writer provided a parallel, not a model. Certainly Hardy's claim that he was a

6. John Crowe Ransom, "Alienation a Century Ago," *Kenyon Review*, XV (Spring, 1953), 336.
7. Quoted in apRoberts, *Arnold and God*, 69.

"meliorist" rather than a pessimist could not have greatly appealed to the young Ransom, who was impressed most of all by the unalterable reality of the world as he knew it. A degree of ambivalence concerning religious matters, however, is still very much evident in some of Ransom's earliest poems, which are about young men who are alternately angry with a cruel and partly evil deity and yet skeptical that anything relating its actual existence can be known. Ransom would later describe Hardy's years immediately following that poet's religious loss along somewhat similar lines: "The ironic disposition of evil [in a poem such as 'The Subalterns'] may look to us like an interim arrangement, while he was collecting his wits and gathering his courage again." It might even have been necessary, Ransom suggests at one point, to allow time for "some transcendent order to assert itself."[8] He himself at least was clearly not inclined to make a hasty decision in such an important matter: he would backslide from, rather than break abruptly with, his family's religious tradition.

And yet one of the most striking aspects of Ransom's development is that the germ of all his later ideas seems to have been present from the very beginning of his childhood. On one occasion, for example, during the closing years of his life, he was to recall his earliest theological confrontation with his father, which was based on his personal perception rather than on any critical reading he might have done at the time. Following a sermon by John James on the natural beauty of God's world, the young Ransom was curious to know "if God would want such beauty disturbed for the benefit of man." Finally exasperated after having all of his replies either rejected or queried further, his father delivered the good-natured rebuke: "Ella, this boy will surely be a lawyer. He would argue with a mile board."[9] For Ransom, the concrete, the immediately perceptible—what he later referred to as "the world's body"—was always primary, though threatened constantly by vain attempts at either its technological or religious transformation. When, therefore, the biblical explanation of how this world came to be the kind of place it actually is—ugly as well as beautiful, filled with pain as well as with happiness—failed him, he was left, not so much with the problem of looking at the world anew, but rather with the need to seek out an alternative interpretation for

8. Young, *Gentleman in a Dustcoat,* 34; John Crowe Ransom, Introduction to Ransom (ed.), *Selected Poems of Thomas Hardy* (New York, 1961), xxxii, xxiv.

9. Young, *Gentleman in a Dustcoat,* 39.

that which he had already experienced. In short, he needed a philosophy.

Following a brilliant undergraduate career at Vanderbilt, however, Ransom set out for Oxford as a Rhodes Scholar in 1910 burdened less with a version of those religious and personal anxieties that were troubling T. S. Eliot on his way to Paris and the Sorbonne in the same year than with a desire to do well in a rather conventionally academic way. Nevertheless, in entertaining the possibility of an eventual career as a philosophy professor at an American university, Ransom must also have had some hope that his study of *Literae Humaniores* would at least suggest answers to the problems of belief he had so far encountered. While his preparation in Latin and Greek had been excellent, his philosophical background left much to be desired: "with the exception of the formal logic (which could not help being a close dialectical discipline) there was not at my college . . . any decent instruction in philosophy which did not consist simply in acquiring the separate knowledges of the systems of famous philosophers." A critical attitude that would have examined the validity of the various systems studied had not been fostered. Much of the reason for Ransom's deficiency in this particular discipline is revealed in a rather amusing anecdote concerning his first meeting with his tutor in philosophy at Christ Church. Asked what text he had used for deductive logic, Ransom replied that the author had been one Noah K. Davis:

"Ah, I don't know the name; but did you do anything else?" And I said, "Well, we had a course in inductive logic." And he said, "What did you read?" And I said, "We had a book by Noah K. Davis." And he said, "A most ubiquitous man." And then he said, "Did you take any other courses?" I said, "Yes, then we had a course in ethics." And he said, "Whom did you read? But please don't say Noah K. Davis." I said, "Noah K. Davis." And he said, "My education is faulty. I don't know Noah K. Davis. But did you take any other courses?" I said, "Yes, then we had a course in psychology." And he said, "I can't bear it, but I feel that you had Noah K. Davis." I said, "Yes." And it was perfectly true that we had had Noah K. Davis, and no other philosopher, living or dead.[10]

Davis had been a philosophy professor at the University of Virginia, and his textbooks were used by Ransom's instructor at Vanderbilt (who assisted in their preparation) on account of their strong religious orthodoxy.

10. John Crowe Ransom, "Strategy for English Studies," *Southern Review*, VI (Autumn, 1940), 228; Young, *Gentleman in a Dustcoat*, 41.

It is with his arrival at Oxford that contemporary evidence for the progress of Ransom's intellectual life becomes available for the first time, though in a rather modest and unsystematic way. His surviving letters to various members of his family show that he was highly successful on both the social and academic scenes. Uniformly self-assured, tending even to a slight primness at times, they certainly betray no hint of religious turmoil. Indeed, what is most striking about them is their casual mention of a wide variety of controversial authors without the least comment on the novelty or unorthodoxy of the writers' views. He refers with surprising frequency, for example, to an essay on Ibsen's ethics which he was preparing for submission to the same editor of the *Methodist Quarterly Review* who had recently been severely admonished for giving excessive attention to modern biblical criticism.

More importantly, however, in the letters specifically addressed to his father, Ransom also outlines the direction in which his own thought was moving. By the end of his period at Oxford, after he had studied in some depth such philosophers as Plato, Aristotle, Hume, Kant, Bosanquet, William James, and Bergson, it was clearly the American pragmatism of James (who had lectured at Oxford in 1908) and John Dewey (whose Jamesian *Studies in Logical Theory* was, according to Ransom, "the most suggestive philosophical work" he knew), rather than the idealism of the still-living F. H. Bradley, that appealed to him (*SL*, 71).[11] Ransom had come to an Oxford that, as Gilbert Ryle has explained, was near the tail end of a transition from the days when philosophical debates were over issues between theologians and antitheologians to those in which "transcendental dictions were becoming unidiomatic . . . as the technicalities of logical theory and scientific method were stiffening the working parlance of philosophers."[12] Still, however much Oxford philosophical instruction has always tended to be informed

11. Ransom named the philosophers listed here in 1920, when, as an assistant professor of English, he petitioned the graduate committee of the university to be allowed to undertake a Ph.D. in philosophy with English and Greek as minor subjects (Ransom to Graduate Committee, October 16, 1920, Vanderbilt University Archives). He did not pursue this degree.

12. Gilbert Ryle, Introduction to A. J. Ayer *et al.*, *The Revolution in Philosophy* (London, 1956), 4. Ryle is referring to his own arrival in Oxford in the mid-1920s, when, according to him, the transition that had begun in the last decades of the nineteenth century was complete. The many references in Ransom's letters to the philosophico-scientific debates he was having with his fellow undergraduates make it clear that the change was well under way during his period there.

and guided by the controversies of the day, as a student in pursuit of a second undergraduate degree Ransom was also required to become familiar with the history of his subject. Thus, for example, writing to his father on February 16, 1913, he noted that:

> The chief bias that obtains at Oxford in Philosophy is toward the historical point of view, the accepted method of treating any subject being to state the successive historical views of it, and accept one of them with modifications, rather than start from the beginning with an independent analysis of the situation. . . . Pragmatism, for instance, has too little historical standing to meet with the minimum of fair treatment at Oxford. Personally, I think that Pragmatism will change the map of philosophy in a generation or so, though it is such a wide term that few people can endorse all the doctrine which has been put forward under it. (SL, 70–71)

Ransom's sympathy in this letter with the pragmatists allies him loosely with the radical shift in British philosophy that had been initiated a few years earlier at Cambridge by G. E. Moore and Bertrand Russell in their revolt against Bradley's form of idealism. Although Moore's objections were based on an appeal to common sense and Russell's on more technical grounds, Russell was to claim that it was really the pragmatist William James who, in the English-speaking world, had been "the greatest influence in the overthrow of German idealism." [13]

The issue here requires some elaboration if only because of the fact that since T. S. Eliot was to do his dissertation research on Bradley's *Appearance and Reality* at both Harvard and Oxford a few years later, there has been a tendency to suppose that Ransom was also inclined toward some form of philosophical idealism when, in fact, his inclination was quite the opposite. Indeed, it has been suggested that even Eliot's dissertation, when read on its own terms rather than in the light of his subsequent spiritual development, provides less a defense of Bradley's philosophy than a pragmatic disillusionment with the ultimate worth of all such ambitious endeavors. In any case, Ransom did not, as one commentator has

13. Bertrand Russell, *Sceptical Essays* (London, 1956), 57. Ransom was an enthusiastic purchaser of the inexpensive books in the Home University Series that had begun to appear in Britain in 1912 and that included Russell's classic *The Problems of Philosophy* among its first publications (SL, 59). His very brief annotations to his Oxford copy of Russell's book, however, suggest that Ransom was not yet fully at ease with this philosopher's "extreme realism" in which mind and consciousness seemed to receive less than their due (this and other books from Ransom's library are in the Vanderbilt University Archives).

suggested, sit under Bradley's tutelage from 1911 to 1913—though for no better reason, perhaps, than that ill health had forced the philosopher to retire from teaching decades earlier; even Eliot, a student at the same college, never met him.[14] Moreover, Dewey's book on logic that Ransom admired had been strongly attacked by Bradley for its skeptical implications and, besides, had appeared in a series that Dewey himself had presented as being "most sharply opposed" to the views of Mill, Lotze, Bosanquet, and Bradley.[15] Nor does Ransom seem to have been significantly influenced by the British philosopher's American counterpart, Josiah Royce of Harvard, who came to Oxford in 1913 to lecture on "Human Nature and Christian Doctrine" and whom Ransom entertained in his capacity as an officer of the American Club (SL, 72).[16] But, more crucially, it was those very aspects of the world that most appealed to Ransom that had disturbed Bradley: its fragmented, disjointed, and irrational particularity. Bradley's Absolute, in which all separation is overcome and all distinctions vanish, was an idea that was quite alien to Ransom's sensibility. William James had characterized this form of absolute idealism as "All are one with God, and with God all is well" and had gone on to criticize it most of all for its implication that evil is apparent rather than real. "The scale of evil," James protested, "defies all human tolerance; and transcendental idealism, in the pages of a Bradley or a Royce, brings us no farther than the book of Job did. . . . A God who can relish such superfluities of horror is no God for human beings to appeal to."[17]

14. F. P. Jarvis, "F. H. Bradley's Appearance and Reality and the Critical Theory of John Crowe Ransom," in Thomas Daniel Young (ed.), John Crowe Ransom: Critical Essays and a Bibliography (Baton Rouge, 1968), 206. See also Richard Wollheim, F. H. Bradley (London, 1969). The philosopher Brand Blanchard, however, a fellow student with Eliot at Merton College in 1914 and 1915, visited the reclusive Bradley and found him quite congenial. See Brand Blanchard, "Eliot at Oxford," Southern Review, XXI (Autumn, 1985), 889–98. An interesting—although perhaps disputable—account of both the substance and contending interpretations of Eliot's dissertation is available in Louis Menand's Discovering Modernism: T. S. Eliot and His Context (New York, 1987), 41–53. Menand also refers to other remarks by Eliot on Bradley and Leibniz as "firmly antitranscendentalist" (48). See in addition Walter Benn Michaels' "Philosophy in Kinkanja: Eliot's Pragmatism," Glyph, VIII (1981), 170–202.

15. George Dykhuizen, The Life and Mind of John Dewey (Carbondale, Ill., 1973), 86; John Dewey, The Middle Works, 1899–1924, ed. Jo Ann Boydston (Carbondale, Ill., 1976), 296.

16. Ransom wrote subsequently that Royce "impressed me very favorably, as contrasted with most of the Oxford philosophers, for being very kind and human" (SL, 74).

17. William James, Pragmatism (Cambridge, Mass., 1975), 70.

Ransom might not have agreed fully with James's conclusion, but he certainly shared his fellow American's belief that the evil in the universe was quite real. To state matters in this way is, of course, to oversimplify Ransom's thinking at the time. It implies, furthermore, that one must be "for" this philosopher and "against" that one as though it were not possible to choose eclectically from among the variety of ideas offered. But even Russell himself greatly admired certain aspects of Bradley's thought and pointed out subsequently that the distinctions between the different schools of philosophy were not always rigid: "William James may be regarded as almost the founder of both realism and pragmatism. Dr. Whitehead's recent books employ the methods of realists in defense of a more or less Bergsonian metaphysic. Many philosophers, not without a considerable show of reason, regard Einstein's doctrines as affording a scientific basis for Kant's belief in the subjectivity of time and space." Likewise, a self-confessed pragmatist such as Ransom, who was always careful to indicate his reservations concerning any specific line of thought, could later refer to at least one aspect of this early period of his life as "my Platonic and metaphysical days" and, in a famous critique of *The Waste Land* in 1923, join together what in retrospect might look like a curious grouping of opposing philosophers: "Since James and Bradley and Bergson, since Kant if we had always had ears to hear, since the Carus Lectures of John Dewey if we only began to listen yesterday, it is borne in upon us that abstract science is incapable of placing the stream of consciousness—the source of all that is—upon the narrow tablets of the [scientific] record."[18] An interest in the stream of consciousness, an emphasis on the rich flux of immediate experience, and an opposition to scientific abstraction were what all of these diverse thinkers had in common and what made them significant in Ransom's ongoing attempt at elaborating a new theory of knowledge that would both account for and replace a shattered Christian cosmology.[19]

18. Russell, *Sceptical Essays*, 55; John Crowe Ransom, "Waste Lands," in Michael Grant (ed.), *T. S. Eliot: The Critical Heritage* (2 vols.; London, 1982), I, 174. Dewey's lectures, delivered in New York in December, 1922, were later expanded and published as *Experience and Nature* (Chicago, 1925).

19. In *The Matrix of Modernism: Pound, Eliot, and Early Twentieth-Century Thought* (Princeton, 1985), Sanford Schwartz explains how Bradley, "his retention of the Absolute notwithstanding . . . belongs in the company of Bergson, James, Nietzsche, and other philosophers who were challenging traditional assumptions about mind and reality" (35). See also Menand's remarks in *Discovering Modernism*, 32–33.

Much the same can be said for the apparent contradiction between the strong interest that Ransom developed in Kant while at
Oxford and his own generally anti-idealist bias. Just as he preferred the materialist emphasis of Aristotle to the abstractionist
thought of Plato, so too it was Kant as awakened from his "dogmatic slumber" and as solver of the problems set by the empiricist
Hume, rather than as precursor of Hegelian idealism, that attracted
Ransom—though Hegel too, as Ransom was later to remark, had
his "pragmatic part" (*SE*, 293). Thus, when Ransom claimed that
he had backslid from his father's faith "even before I came upon
Kant the Transcendentalist," what he appears to have meant was
that this philosopher had shaken whatever beliefs he had left in orthodox Christianity while at the same time providing him with a
possible solution to the religious crisis (*WB*, 376). While Kant had
indeed attacked the traditional proofs for the existence of God—
"the concept of an absolutely necessary Being is a concept of pure
reason, that is, a mere idea, the objective reality of which is by no
means proved by the fact that reason requires it"—he had at the
same time answered Hume's skepticism concerning the existence
of metaphysical entities with the argument that it was necessary
for the mind to posit such entities in order to function in the world
at all.[20] The conclusion for Ransom, though no record exists indicating that he stated it at the time, would appear to have been that
the essential "facts" of Christianity that had been demolished by
the higher critics of the Bible could now be reconstituted as necessary fictions, though in so doing he was, of course, departing from
his father's faith—and indeed from Kant's pietistic belief—in the
objective truth of religious revelation.

Ransom's strong inclination toward empiricism, then—of which
pragmatism was a particular development—seems to have been
tempered somewhat by the remnants of an idealism that was the
secular counterpart of his original religious convictions.[21] But, with

20. John Crowe Ransom, "Art Worries the Naturalists," in *Beating the Bushes: Selected Essays, 1941–1970* (New York, 1972), 103; Immanuel Kant, *The Critique of Pure
Reason*, trans. F. Max Müller (London, 1896), 477; John Crowe Ransom, *God Without
Thunder: An Unorthodox Defense of Orthodoxy* (New York, 1930; rpr. Hamden, Conn.,
1965), 216, hereinafter cited parenthetically by page number in the text.
21. It has been remarked on a number of occasions that idealism was often seen
as a potential antidote to the disintegration of religious belief that empiricism threatened. Anthony Manser, for example, has argued that Benjamin Jowett introduced
Hegel's philosophy to Oxford for such purposes (*Bradley's Logic* [Oxford, 1983], 10).

some skepticism, he took it upon himself to attend Oxford's first experimental-psychology laboratory under William McDougall and even to write essays on the subject (*SL*, 42). And, while Eliot in Paris in 1911 attending the Collège de France was finding Bergson's philosophical use of biology and psychology "suspect," Ransom was reading that same philosopher at Oxford and storing up those comments on the physiology of the brain with which he would one day attempt to give a naturalistic explanation for Eliot's "still moments" of religious insight (*WB*, 365). Above all, he was—as he wrote in a letter to his father concerning the difficulties of Kant's *Critique of Pure Reason*—doing some thinking on his own and had "a few ideas which seem to me original and more or less sound."[22] The ideas in question, which appear to have been specifically concerned with morals and poetics and which were inspired by his reading of Kant's other critiques also, can be seen as the first glimmerings of a new, secular faith (though he would probably have vigorously contested the description at the time) to replace the old one that his studies at Oxford had finally extinguished.

22. Lyndall Gordon, *Eliot's Early Years* (New York, 1977), 38; John Crowe Ransom to John James Ransom, January 14, 1912, in Ellene Ransom Papers, Tennessee State Library and Archives.

2

Poems About "God"

Perhaps what strikes one most about Ransom as he prepared to return to the United States from Oxford in 1913 is his general buoyancy. Certainly that is the case whenever one thinks of a morbid Eliot in contrast. For Ransom, the pain of religious loss may already have become "chronic and low-grade," for there is no sense whatever that he was suffering Arnoldian distress over the issue or that the loss was as traumatic as it had been for James and Dewey decades earlier. On the contrary, for several years afterwards Ransom was to take an almost wicked delight in slyly shocking the conventional beliefs of his more orthodox friends and students. Becoming in 1914 an instructor in Vanderbilt's English— rather than philosophy—department at a time when it was still possible to obtain an academic position for which one had not been specifically trained (and after toying briefly with the idea of practicing journalism in New York and after spending a year as a classics master at a prep school in Connecticut), Ransom would employ procedures learned from Bergson and the British empiricists to deflate the wilder philosophical and theological speculations of some of his Nashville friends when they met together in the discussion group later to become known as the Fugitives. Donald Davidson, first a student and later a colleague of Ransom's at Vanderbilt, had introduced Ransom to this lively circle, the membership of which consisted of "Southernized Jews and art-minded Gentiles" from both university and city.[1] Whatever slight exaggeration may be implied in that description, the coming together of a set of at least relatively unconventional minds who were consciously fleeing—as

1. Louise Cowan, *The Fugitive Group: A Literary History* (Baton Rouge, 1959), 17; Donald Davidson, *Southern Writers in the Modern World* (Athens, Ga., 1958), 13.

they subsequently explained the matter—the "high-caste Brahmins of the Old South" was to provide Ransom with the almost perfect forum for his ongoing intellectual development.

At the time he joined the group, Ransom had just published an essay in the *Yale Review* in which he applied concepts drawn from moral philosophy to a contemporary issue: distinguishing between the Platonic and Aristotelian notions of social justice, he argued that the German and British positions in the European war might be considered to be of equal merit. Now, however, though the early discussions among the Fugitives (or, strictly speaking, pre-Fugitives) also tended to have a strong philosophical bias, their interest in the vers libre controversy—Frost's "playing tennis with the net down"—seems to have provoked Ransom to move in what at first might appear to be a rather different direction: he attempted to write a poem and to do so in the free-verse style. But that his direction was not at all different from what it had been before is seen from the fact that the poem was to have as its theme one of the central concerns of his long-standing religious and philosophical preoccupations. "Sunset" is about the incomprehension between a man who is impressed by the beauty of this world and a woman who sees such beauty merely as a reflection of God:

> Two people never sat like us by a fence of cedar rails
> On a still evening
> And looked at such fat fields.
> To me it is beautiful enough,
> I am stirred,
> I say grand and wonderful, and grow adjectival,
> But to you
> It is God.

After some further observations in the same vein and the remark that the woman's look "terrifies" him, the lover concludes that he will, however, simply wait until she "And her strange eyes / Come home from God." [2]

Ransom's poem is extraordinarily flat; it offers an almost too-clear statement of the conflict between immanence and transcendence, between the "body" of this world and the insubstantiality of the other one, that was to occupy him throughout his life. But

2. John Crowe Ransom, "The Question of Justice," *Yale Review*, IV (July, 1915), 684–98, and *Poems About God* (New York, 1919), 13–16, hereinafter cited parenthetically by page number in the text.

what is most significant is that in "Sunset" religion—in its conventional variety, at least—far from being defended, is conceived of as an abstraction that takes away from the fullness of this world. Indeed, it is as though Ransom's new faith had initially set him in direct opposition to traditional religion.

Robert Penn Warren (who was not to join the Fugitives until several years later) has speculated that Ransom first became a poet at the relatively late age of twenty-seven because poetry was the only medium through which he could deal with the emotional as well as intellectual impact of the conflicts that were engaging his mind: "If the theme of the poetry had been, we can argue, of merely intellectual urgency, it would seem logical, in the light of his own special philosophical training and interest, to suppose that he would have approached the issue by way of prose speculation. In any case, the issue was not . . . merely of intellectual and professional concern; it had been, and was being, lived into. . . . From this the poetry would spring because poetry gave the only way to deal with the issue." [3] If Warren's observation is correct, however, it applies more to the poems that Ransom was to write in the 1920s than to those that immediately followed "Sunset" and that were to make up the collection entitled *Poems About God*, which was published in New York in 1919 on the recommendation of Robert Frost. Or, rather, it might be said that Ransom had already "lived into" and resolved— emotionally at least—the issues he was dealing with in these early poems even before he came to write them.

Although Robert Graves as well as Robert Frost admired Ransom's first book, for several decades he himself refused to reprint any of its contents. And were it not for the fact that the themes of these poems shed considerable light on his early religious development, it would be better for the most part to follow his own example. One of the problems of the poems is, as Warren has pointed out, that the most common persona in them is that of a Tennessee farmboy and that "what a farm boy might say is not what we will permit a twenty-eight-year-old scholar to say, and we don't quite know who is talking." The result is that the treatment of "a great issue often seems merely absurd, merely bathetic." [4] Ransom himself put the

3. Robert Penn Warren, "Notes on the Poetry of John Crowe Ransom at His Eightieth Birthday," *Kenyon Review*, XXX (1968), 322–23.

4. *Ibid.*, 326. Warren also suggests that Ransom may have been attempting to imitate the poems in Housman's *A Shropshire Lad*.

matter more acutely in 1969 when he described the collection as characterized by "blatant and inconsistent theologizing."[5]

Certainly, the title of the volume, *Poems About God*, would have been more accurately rendered as *Poems About "God,"* for, as Ransom notes in the introduction, which he composed afterwards in France in 1918 when he was serving as an artillery officer in World War I, it is not a personal God that the poems are dealing with but rather a *term*, "the most poetic of all terms possible": "a term always being called into requisition during the great moments of the soul, now in tones of love, and now indignantly; and was the very last word that a man might say when standing in the presence of that ultimate mystery to which all our great experiences reduce" (vi–vii).[6] Ransom states that his intention is to "treat rather systematically" a variety of occasions on which this term is used among common Americans, though he adds immediately that he also is to be included among such users: "I very quickly ruled that I should consider only those situations as suitable in which I could imagine myself pronouncing the name God sincerely and spontaneously, never by that way of routine which is death to the aesthetic and religious emotions" (vii). In his own echoing of Kant and Schleiermacher, however, Ransom overlooks the problem that most "common Americans," rightly or wrongly, do not think of themselves as invoking a mere term on those occasions on which they use the word *God;* he himself probably did not use it in such a fashion in his Tennessee youth. And he simply sidesteps the issue when he observes that though God's name is taken here "in ways that are not the ways of the fathers," there are many mountains on which the deity may be worshiped in this world (vii).

Then again, it is hard to see how it could be asserted that God's name is being invoked "in tones of love," for almost all of the poems are indignantly critical either of the deity itself or, more ac-

5. John Crowe Ransom, *Selected Poems* (3rd. ed.; New York, 1969), 112, hereinafter cited parenthetically by page number in the text as *SP*.

6. Ransom's references to God, god(s), the deity, and the divine seem highly inconsistent at first glance and certainly do not follow customary Judeo-Christian usage. This is partly because, when writing about the divinity, he has equally in mind the classical gods of Greece and Rome, the God of the Christians, and the gods of the various Oriental religions. For Ransom, God is a totally unknown Power not to be identified with any particular religious description of him—indeed, he sometimes refers to God as "it." In general, I have tried to reflect the tone of Ransom's usage: thus *divine* and *deity* are not capitalized, and *God* is often used where a more scrupulous commentator might prefer *god*.

curately, of those who are foolish enough to worship it. What is most curious of all is Ransom's attitude in the introduction to the author of the poems—his own self of just over a year earlier. It is understandable that he should admit that his recent experience in the war has broadened his view so that he can "actually look back upon those antebellum accomplishments with the eye of an impartial spectator, or at most with a fatherly tenderness." But when he writes that he now finds himself "thinking sometimes that the case about God may not be quite as desperate as the young poet chooses to believe," though he is "deeply engaged" by the "downright evident honesty of the young man" who has written the poems and will never think of suppressing a single one of them, the impression left is of a rather maladroit attempt at distancing himself from an embarrassingly unsophisticated oeuvre (v).

It may be that Vivienne Koch is overstating the case when she judges that the poems in this collection are "transparently autobiographical."[7] Still, they are self-referential to a large extent and reflect with "downright evident honesty" progressive stages of Ransom's religious evolution. The initial output of a poetic career that had begun with three or four poems written "in three or four different moods" in fact covers a broad period of time in the author's life, so that at least some of the theological inconsistencies that Ransom himself later recognized simply mirror his own youthful confusion on the issue. In any case, *Poems About God* is essentially retrospective.

The kind of conflict between familial piety and youthful skepticism that occurs in "Noonday Grace," for example, is reminiscent of those early exchanges with his father that Ransom was to recall so vividly in his old age. The narrator is a young boy who is mildly satirical of his father's traditional practice of thanking God at mealtime. He himself, on the other hand, prays "with total fervency":

> Thank you, good Lord, for dinner-time!
> Gladly I come from the sweat and grime
> To play in your Christian pantomime.

The boy seems to be still in pantomime mood when he thanks God "who made the garden grow, / Who took upon himself to know / That we loved vegetables so." His tone, however, suggests that he

---

7. Vivienne Koch, "The Achievement of John Crowe Ransom," in Young (ed.), *John Crowe Ransom: Critical Essays*, 116.

does not quite believe all of this, an assumption that is confirmed very shortly afterwards:

> Sunday the preacher droned a lot
> About a certain whether or not:
> Is God the universal friend,
> And if men pray can he attend
> To each man's individual end?

The boy goes on to offer his own answer to this question, an answer that criticizes the lack of elevation in the desires and aspirations of most believers:

> They pray for individual things,
> Give thanks for little happenings,
> But isn't his sweep of mighty wings
> Meant more for business of kings
> Than pulling small men's petty strings?

He questions the preacher, a "valiant democrat," as to how an infinite God could concern himself with mere "creeping man." The two-line stanza that immediately follows is placed within quotation marks and would appear to be the minister's response: "The greatest of all, his sympathy, / His kindness, reaching down to me." The boy, however, translates this lofty consolation to "Like mother, he [God] finds it his greatest joy / To have big dinners for his boy" (6–10). Overall, therefore, the narrator seems to disagree with the ridiculously self-oriented nature of much Christian piety, though for the moment he himself does not express any doubts concerning the existence of the deity or its generally benign disposition toward man: the narrator simply has a far more elevated concept of such a divine being than most believers.

The speaker in "Grace" is probably the boy of the previous poem, now grown up, for he still remembers his "mother's pickles and pies." If so, then his satiric vision has grown apace. The poem opens with a direct accusation:

> Who is it beams the merriest
> At killing a man, the laughing one?
> You are the one I nominate,
> God of the rivers of Babylon.

The example he gives of such a killing concerns a hired man with whom he once worked. During intervals of rest, he would lead the hired man on by singing a gospel tune such as "Down at the cross my Savior died," to which the man would respond, "There did I bury my sin and pride." The narrator suddenly pauses to comment: "Sinful pride of a hired man! / Out of a hired woman born!" The poor man's self-criticism is just as inappropriate as the gratitude of the father "past his taste for cookery" in "Noonday Grace." The narrator continues, "I'm thinking now how he was saved / One day while plowing in the corn," so that one can almost hear the ironic inflection on the word *saved*. The hired man in fact fell in a furrow while his horse went "marching blindly on" thinking of his well-provided stall. The deity's response is one of amusement:

> And God shone on in merry mood,
> For it was a foolish kind of sprawl,
> And I found a hulk of heaving meat
> That wouldn't answer me at all.
> And a fresh breeze made the young corn dance
> To a bright green, glorious carnival.

This detached, even sadistic, attitude of God is ironically commended by the poet at the time of writing, though he confesses that on the occasion itself he was "forward and untamed" and reacted in quite a different way, protesting:

> I will not worship wickedness
> Though it be God's—I am ashamed!
> For all his mercies God be thanked
> But for his tyrannies be blamed!
> He shall not have my love alone,
> With loathing too his name is named.

In the final scene of the poem, God's praises fill the earth, the melodious song broken only by a solitary crow that caws, "not knowing how to sigh" (18–23). This concluding line has an awkwardness that may or may not have been intended, but one that well reflects the narrator's disordered feelings at the time of the original experience. Or, as Ransom was to remark years later concerning the flatness of the last line of one of Emily Dickinson's poems: "Its blankness cancels out the expostulation we had expected, and pure contingency replaces the vicious agent we would have blamed [for a death], and there is nothing rational to be said. Who is going to blame a fact?" [8] Throughout "Grace," criticism ap-

---

8. John Crowe Ransom, "Emily Dickinson: A Poet Restored," in Richard B. Sewall (ed.), *Emily Dickinson: A Collection of Critical Essays* (Englewood Cliffs, 1963), 92.

pears to be as much focused on the God who has created this harsh world as on those Christians who are naïve enough not to recognize the discrepancy between their belief in a benign deity and their actual experience of life; thus the narrator has advanced to a further stage of religious skepticism, though one that he has not as yet satisfactorily expressed.

"Moonlight" continues in the same accusatory tone, while "Geometry" suggests that man might have designed the world better than God has. The narrator of the latter poem employs several adjectives that are not usually associated with the deity:

> He still plants on as crazily
> As in his drivelling infancy. . . .
>
> Hickory shoots unnumbered rise,
> Sallow and wasting themselves in sighs,
> Children begot at a criminal rate
> In the sight of a God that is profligate.

The remedy that the ordered mind of the narrator offers is to

> Imagine what a pretty thing
> The slightest landscape-gardening
> Had made of God's neglected wood! . . .
>
> An easy thing to improve on God,
> Simply the knowing of even from odd,
> Simply to count and then dispose
> In patterns everybody knows,
> Simply to follow curve and line
> In geometrical design

He realizes, however, that such speculative improvements would eventually be frustrated by a temperamental divinity:

> But from my window I have seen
> The noblest patch of quivering green
> Lashed till it never quivered again.
> God had a fit of temper then,
> And spat shrill wind and lightning out
> At twinges of some godly gout.
> But as for me, I keep indoors
> Whenever he starts his awful roars.
> What can one hope of a crazy God
> But lashings from an aimless rod?
>
> (27–30)

The anecdote recounted in the previous chapter concerning Ransom's questioning of his father's sermon suggests, of course, that

Ransom himself did not hold the views expressed by the narrator of this poem. But even if the poem is read as an ironic criticism of man's presumption rather than of God's arbitrariness (and an early presentation of one of Ransom's major themes), nevertheless it also strongly implies that the world is indeed a harsh, bitter place and thus raises serious questions about the ultimate reason for this circumstance. Moreover, whatever the degree of irony involved here, Ransom's own interest in geometric gardening allows one to surmise that he, too, sometimes felt a similar temptation to improve on the ways of God.[9]

The poems that immediately follow "Geometry" are more diffuse in their development of the collection's central theme. A parson "Thinks he's preached the doubters down / And old men never tell" ("Under the Locusts," 37–38). The narrator of "November" is condemned by his mother to marry a pious girl who "swallows Christian doctrine straight" so that he is led to rue the ways of God (50–52). The little girl in "A Christmas Colloquy" who "hates the sound of piety" is required to listen to the story of Jesus when she would much rather hear about Santa Claus (53–56). "The Power of God" has echoes of "Geometry": the poet claims that if the power of God were his, he would summon his ministers who are "stony and reconciled" to the suffering of the world and arrange to see that women are better looked after by his providence (57–59). The speaker in "The Resurrection" is skeptical of the ideas of those who believe in the possibility announced in the poem's title. Passing stooped old men on the highway, he feels

> sick and shamed that Heaven has been
> So clumsy with the inelastic clay!
> "What pretty piece of hope then have you spun,
> My old defeated traveler," I say,
> "That keeps you marching on? For I have none.
> I have looked often and I have not found
> Old men bowed low who ever rose up sound."
>
> (60)

9. George Lanning lived near Ransom's house on the Kenyon campus: "At the rear is Mr. Ransom's garden—everything separated according to its nature, and lined up firmly and confined squarely. 'It's not what I'd call a garden,' a neighbor says every summer. 'I wish John would mix things up a little, and stop putting all his plants in *rows*.'" See George Lanning, "Ransom as Editor," in Young (ed.), *John Crowe Ransom: Critical Essays*, 210–11.

In "April," God restores the world after the emaciation of winter only because he wishes to hear his own praise again (64). "Prayer" criticizes a poor woman for her unnecessary self-abasement before a rather distant and foolish divinity:

> She would not keep at home, the foolish woman,
> She would not mind her precious girls and boys,
> She had to go, for it was Sunday morning,
> Down the hot road and to the barren pew
> And there abuse her superannuate knees
> To make a prayer.
>
> (67–68)

The woman's attitude is considered to be just as inappropriate as that of the hired man in "Grace."

The final poem in the collection, "Sickness," is reminiscent of Hardy's "The Subalterns," for here God seems to be less than all-powerful. God is in attendance at the bedside of "The toughest carcass in the town": "See, I am not that Scriptural! / A lesser, kinder God instead." The reader is told that God cannot "do much for his countryman," implying that he at least belongs to the same imperfect world that people inhabit. He is, however, able to save the dying man from what are referred to as "certain dreams." Among these "dreams" is the notion that being treated like "a bruised, a beaten slave" is a redemptive sign from "God's white hand" (74–76). The criticism implied here is of those who see the suffering of this world as a mysterious token of God's beneficence: such a "dream" is spared the reader by a more realistic depiction of the actual situation, in which a helpless God is himself without recourse in these grim circumstances. The conclusion seems to be that it is quite illusory to think that there is an all-powerful being from whom salvation either in this life or in the next can be expected.

Poems About God provides considerable insight into Ransom's early thinking on religion. At least one prominent critic has made the puzzling observation that "the few outbursts of anger against the injustice of God are smothered by other passages of conventional piety." Quite the contrary: nowhere in these poems is conventional piety commended. Indeed, throughout the entire volume Ransom is almost unrelentingly critical of all aspects of the religious phenomenon, though several of the criticisms are inconsistent with one another. Perhaps the best way of looking at this early work, then, is in terms of a remark with which Ransom was to preface his selection of Thomas Hardy's verse some forty years later: "As if to allow in advance for the failure of human speculations, including his own, Hardy often gives them a sporting or rowdy turn which makes them comic in their irony."[10] In a recent criticism of the peculiar selection that Ransom made of Hardy's poems, Donald Davie argues that this observation is more applicable to the American's own work than to that of the British poet.[11] But, quite apart from these considerations, the overwhelming impression of the collection is that it is the output of an author who has little respect for the traditional Christian pieties but who also has not yet adequately developed the elements of an alternative philosophy.

10. John L. Stewart, *The Burden of Time: The Fugitives and Agrarians* (Princeton, 1965), 214; Ransom (ed.), *Selected Poems of Thomas Hardy*, x.

11. Donald Davie, *Thomas Hardy and British Poetry* (New York, 1972), 30. Davie goes on to point out that the Spirit of Irony that Ransom would wish to be more prominent in Hardy is a characteristic rather of Housman's poetry; in Hardy, the scientific humanist, "the Spirit of Pity, not Irony, would always have the last word."

3

A Calmer Skepticism

"I had no such experience as you did in the War," the former first
lieutenant J. C. Ransom of the American Expeditionary Force commented to the much wounded Robert Graves some years after his
own return from France in 1919 (*SL*, 138). He had come back to a
little local disturbance, however, for publication of *Poems About God*
had caused a stir in Nashville among several of his father's clerical
friends who were shocked by its contents, though John James
himself remained largely sympathetic, even commenting on and
emending a number of the individual poems. Ironically, perhaps,
the period of Ransom's attack on the divinity as such was already
over by this time, and what remained now was to account philosophically for the religious phenomenon and to criticize specific
untruths of its teachings.

The reconvened Fugitive circle, meanwhile, was moving more
and more in the direction of the writing of poetry. Even so, when
the young Allen Tate was invited to join the group as late as November, 1921, he found it more philosophical and linguistic than literary, its core members gathered around the chaise longue of the
"mystic" and "Rosicrucian" Sidney Hirsch, a Nashvillian of Jewish
background who had traveled widely in Europe and in Asia, where
he had met a number of the leading writers and artists of the day,
and of whose intellectual eclecticism Ransom was especially defla-
tionary. The group's poetry—which had to undergo the vigorous
criticism of its members—was certainly dominated by philosophical and religious themes. Soon the Fugitives had a sufficient number written to suggest the need for a magazine in which to publish
them. Ransom's contribution, the opening poem of the first issue,
bore the startlingly naked title "Ego" and revealed that its author
saw himself as a kind of Socratic gadfly:

> You have heard something muttered in my scorn:
> "A little learning addleth this man's wit,
> He crieth on our dogmas Counterfeit!
> And no man's bubble 'scapeth his sharp thorn; . . ."
>
> Friends! come acquit me of that stain of pride:
> Much has been spoken solemnly together,
> And you have heard my heart; so answer whether
> I am so proud a Fool, and godless beside.

Although the last line suggests that Ransom's attitude toward religion was known among his friends to be more complex than some of his critics had allowed, a local reviewer was quick to point out that the "incongruous" nom de plume "Roger Prim" did not at all conceal the fact that the author of "Ego" was also responsible for "some of the more rabid 'Poems About God.'"[1]

Two of the other three poems that Ransom published in the first issue of the *Fugitive* were also about religion. "The Handmaidens" is more or less a revision of "The Power of God" from his 1919 collection, updated with a few references to the war in France. "Night Voices," the first of many poems on biblical figures, is of greater interest. Although its diction and syntax are awkward and archaic, and the thrust of its argument consequently less direct than one might wish, the poem expresses an aspect of the religious issue that was always of central importance for Ransom—and one that had only been hinted at in "The Resurrection."

"Night Voices" opens with the "youths" Nicodemus and Jesus withdrawing after dark, "Unseen they hoped of all the synagogue," to engage in a "duologue." The former then accuses Jesus of having misled the populace with false hopes of an afterlife, which Jesus himself is no more likely to enjoy than they are:

> I have the whole hearsay,
> They titled thee a little god today.
> But didst thou promise to annul the tomb,
> Complaisant with that frightened breed to whom
> Thou fellowest in clay?

Jesus replies with equal vigor:

> I sped their tremulous hope
> For pity of a darkling horoscope.
> For thou art Nicodemus, and thy sect

1. Cowan, *The Fugitive Group*, 38; John Crowe Ransom, "Ego," *Fugitive*, I (April, 1922), 3–4; Cowan, *The Fugitive Group*, 54.

> Hath schooled them so funereal, O stiff-necked,
> Ye stinted all their scope.

Nicodemus remains unconvinced and points to the reality of death, which no amount of hope can dispel:

> Friend, these lies profit not
> When carcasses so visibly do rot.
> As well run forth and cry there is no Rome,
> Still would the legionary scourge them home
> Whom they had fain forgot.

The reply this time is that the "lie" of belief in man's resurrection serves to make the people happier and hence is justified:

> Nay, this lie lasteth more,
> And maketh the mortal mark bite not so sore.
> Our Jewry is fanatic, and I said,
> "In three days must each tomb unclasp his dead!"
> Nor heard such joy before.

Although the poem reaches no conclusion as to who has the stronger argument, it does present the hope of personal immortality as a perennial human inclination that has little real likelihood of fulfillment—a theme that Ransom was to sound time after time in his subsequent writings.[2]

"During the *Fugitive* days of my fourth decade," Ransom confessed in 1969, "I was at great pains to suppress my feelings in what I wrote. I was both sensitive and sentimental as a boy; and I did not like that boyishness in my adult poems" (*SP*, 146). This comment alone is perhaps sufficient to explain Ransom's adoption of a variety of personae in his poems of the early 1920s, thus dispensing with the need to investigate how his particular practice relates, for example, to Eliot's theory of the impersonality of the modern artist.[3] Although Ransom had been introduced to the work of the French symbolists in the interval between the war's end and his return home, he was never part of the resultant modernist movement of T. H. Hulme, Pound, Eliot, and Joyce in either its artistic or its

---

2. John Crowe Ransom, "Night Voices," *Fugitive*, I (April, 1922), 10–11.
3. Sanford Schwartz has pointed out a number of complications in this theory: for example, while Eliot generally recommends the "suspension of personality" for the artist, he also "talks about the impersonal conventions that obscure our personal feelings" (*The Matrix of Modernism*, 69).

religious dimension in anything like the way that Tate was. Indeed, even at this "poetic" stage in his career, Ransom is still much better understood against the background of contemporary developments in British and American philosophy—a subject in which he applied to enter a Ph.D. program as late as 1920—than in terms of a twentieth-century literature the apparent formlessness of which he consistently opposed. So, without claiming that every idea in Ransom's poems of the 1920s is directly attributable to the author himself, one may reasonably suppose that those ideas that keep recurring are expressions of his fundamental philosophical preoccupations at the time, or even, if one wishes, of his consciously "suppressed" feelings on these issues. "There must not be a trace of the expository philosophical method, but nevertheless the substance of the philosophical conclusion must be there for the intelligent reader," he wrote to Tate in 1922 in a sustained—and apparently pointed—criticism of Eliot's poetry. "The artist can't stay off this necessity—can't hold aloof, be the impartial spectator, the colorless medium of information, the carrier of a perfectly undirected passion, the Know-Nothing from Missouri" (SL, 115).

Tate has dated Ransom's transition to a "mature" style from "Necrological," a poem that appeared as early as the second issue of the *Fugitive*. Its theme is similar to that of "Night Voices," but its execution is more satisfying. Based on a medieval account of the death of Charles the Bold, the poem concerns a friar who, disturbed in his sleep, steals away from his monastery to visit the scene of a recent battle. He arrives to find that "the heroes' bosoms were whitely bare," though "Not all were white; some gory and fabulous / Whom the sword had pierced and then the gray wolf eaten." The friar's initial response to this grim sight is to reason "that heroes' flesh was thus." But further contemplation of the scene finally leads the Carmelite to sit with bowed head on a hill,

> Riddling, riddling, and lost in a vast surmise,
> So still that he likened himself unto those dead
> Whom the kites of Heaven solicited with sweet cries.[4]

Religious explanations fail in the actual battlefield with its mutilated dead; the friar's sensibility is stunned, and he lapses into a

---

4. John Crowe Ransom, "Necrological," *Fugitive*, I (June, 1922), 62–63. In the 1969 version, the rather intense "Riddling, riddling, and lost in a vast surmise" becomes the much more sedate "As under a riddle, and in a deep surmise" (*SP*, 42–43).

state of numbed silence. Unlike Christ in "Night Voices," he cannot easily have recourse to a comforting but ultimately vain promise. By using the persona of the friar, Ransom indicates his own
mature attitude, his distancing of himself from his religious loss
even as he finds for it a more powerful expression. Emotionally
and intellectually, he has moved from anger to silence, from bitter
rejection to agnostic puzzlement.

Mature is not only a word that is applied by the critics to Ransom's
best verse but one that he himself used again and again during the
1920s and that represents a significant advance in his understanding of the human condition. In his disparaging review of *The Waste
Land* in 1923, for example, Ransom considers that the poem "takes
a number of years out of this author's history, restores him intellectually to his minority," because there is not "a single occasion
where his context is as mature as the quotation which he inserts
into it." [5] And in a reference to the same subject a couple of years
later, Ransom makes a revealingly acerbic inquiry about a well-
known scene from the New Testament:

> For on the face of it, there seems nothing stranger than the notion that
> wisdom comes out of the mouth of a child. Where did he get it? The
> apocryphal authorities tell many legends about the miracles that the Holy
> Child performed to the discomfiture of his elders; but not one of them
> goes as far as that miracle of sober Scripture, which occurred when
> Jesus removed himself from the company of his parents, went into the
> temple, and confounded his elders with his wisdom, both asking and
> answering questions. Literature never suffered a greater loss than when
> the chronicler refused to report circumstantially these discussions. What
> was his understanding of the imagery of the Songs of Solomon? Or of
> Aristotle's conception of the function of God?   (*SE*, 29)

The mature mind that Ransom recommends is characterized by
an ironic stance toward life, a rejection of romantic hope, and melancholy, and youthful arrogance in favor of a more detached contemplation. Nevertheless, the old attitudes linger on, transformed,
so that, as Warren notes, the "irony—the index of distance, the
mark of uninvolvement—mak[es] the tenderness, the involvement, possible." [6] Thus, for example, the early poem "Grace" offered both a strong condemnation of a cruel deity and a bitter, but

---

5. Ransom, "Waste Lands," in Grant (ed.), *T. S. Eliot: The Critical Heritage*, I, 178.
6. Warren, "Notes on the Poetry of John Crowe Ransom at His Eightieth Birthday," 329.

unsubtle, ironic comment on that deity's attitude toward the death of the hired man:

> And really, is it not a gift
> To smile and be divinely gay,
> To rise above a circumstance
> And smile distressing scenes away?

In later poems such as "Bells for John Whiteside's Daughter," "Dead Boy," and "Janet Waking," however, the irony is directed not at the injustice of the deity or the cruelty of the universe but at the narrator himself, so that he is made aware of the tragic circumstances of life in which there is no villain to accuse. When "a transmogrifying bee" drones down and poisons Janet's pet hen, the little girl is described as

> Kneeling on the wet grass, crying her brown hen
> (Translated far beyond the prayers of men)
> To rise and walk upon it.
>
> And weeping fast as she had breath
> Janet implored us, "Wake her from her sleep!"
> And would not be instructed in how deep
> Was the forgetful kingdom of death.[7]

Robert Pinsky has suggested that "if the cruel archness of these lines . . . is not directed against the little girl and her pet, they must be directed backwards at the grave poet who expects more from life than these simple facts, and who feels bound to speech."[8] Perhaps one should qualify this remark with the rider that Ransom himself expected no more from life than the simple facts he reported.

Many of the poems Ransom wrote at this time deal with man's mortality, the circumscribed possibilities of life, or the great, unbreachable silence that surrounds human existence. If earlier Ransom had sometimes railed against the injustices of the deity, now he seems to perceive that there is nothing—no person or power—to rail against. It is not surprising, therefore, that in the same essay in which Randall Jarrell links Ransom's poems to Mother Goose, he

7. John Crowe Ransom, "Janet Waking," *Fugitive*, IV (September, 1925), 86. In the *Selected Poems* version, Janet's brown hen has been "(Translated far beyond the daughters of men)," suggesting that by the late 1960s Ransom was much less obviously preoccupied with traditional theological matters than he had been in the 1920s (*SP*, 12).

8. Robert Pinsky, "Hardy, Ransom, Berryman: A 'Curious Air,'" *Agenda*, X (Spring–Summer, 1972), 96.

also alludes to their similarity to the "queer fabulous allegories" of Kafka (an author whom Ransom liked), for whose protagonist in *The Castle* no message ever arrives.[9] The world of Ransom's mature poetry is marked by the complete absence of an omnipotent overseer rather than by the presence of a malignant tyrant.

Far from being a simple pessimist, however, Ransom has the positive intention of making the reader face up to the sobering facts of existence without having recourse to the kind of consolation traditionally offered by religious belief. It is especially significant in this regard that his many poems on death have a somewhat different background than might appear at first. All of them are motivated by a philosophic purpose that he had entertained certainly when composing *Poems About God* and probably long before that. The genesis of "Bells for John Whiteside's Daughter" illustrates the matter particularly well. Ransom told his biographer that the poem had been suggested to him while watching a little girl from a neighbor's house at play on a street nearby: he had imagined what it would be like were she to die.[10] So, in the poem, the child's "speed" and "lightness" as she scuttles the lazy geese are abruptly brought to an end:

> But now go the bells, and we are ready,
> In one house we are sternly stopped
> To say we are vexed at her brown study,
> Lying so primly propped.
> *(SP, 7)*

"Bells for John Whiteside's Daughter," then, is not a memorial for a neighbor's child's actual death but an exploration of man's vexation in the face of the inevitable outcome of life. Ransom stated his purposes clearly in a letter to Tate in 1927: "My object as a poet might be something like the following, though I won't promise to stick by my analysis: (1) I want to find the Experience that is in the common actuals; (2) I want this experience to carry (by association of course) the dearest possible values to which we have attached ourselves; (3) I want to face the disintegration or nullification of these values as calmly and religiously as possible" (*SL*, 168–69). Crudely stated, the little girl is an instance of the "common actuals" that have "the dearest possible value" for human beings; her death, therefore,

---

9. Randall Jarrell, *Poetry and the Age* (New York, 1953), 102, 109.
10. Author's conversation with Thomas Daniel Young, November 15, 1983.

forces man to confront the cruel facts of life, and he does so "religiously," not by entertaining vain hopes of future bliss, but rather by remaining stoically calm in these "vexing" circumstances.

Ransom is engaged in the same process in a poem such as "Vision by Sweetwater," in which the boy's idyllic "dream of ladies sweeping by / The willows, clouds, deep meadowgrass" is intruded upon—and he is made "old suddenly"—by "the scream / From one of the white throats which it hid among" (SP, 27). Again Warren has hit upon the elusive point that the poem is implying: "When the poem comes to rest on the word *among*, the fact that the source of the particular scream (which throat?) is unknown is emphasized. The scream belongs, in one sense, not merely to a particular girl, a particular white throat, but could belong to any; and this is a way of saying that it belongs to all, and will, in the end, in the course of life, leap from each and all." [11]

The necessary counterpart to this strategy was to criticize Christians in specific ways for their failure to face such evident, if unpleasant, realities. Ransom continued to do precisely that in several of his poems. The bantering rhyme and rhythm of "Our Two Worthies," for example, almost belie the poem's serious claim that the Christian religion appeals to the abstractive side of man's nature, the side of him that is unwilling to embrace the beauty and ugliness of this world and that seeks refuge in the promise of supernatural rewards:

> Jesus proclaimed the truth.
> Paul's missionary tooth
> Shredded it fine, and made a paste,
> No particle going to waste,
> Kneaded it and caked it
> And buttered it and baked it
> (And indeed all but digested
> While Jesus went to death and rested)
> Into a marketable compound
> Ready to lay on any wound,
> Meet to prescribe to our distress
> And feed unto our emptiness.

> And this is how the Pure Idea
> Became our perfect panacea,
> Both external and internal
> And supernal and infernal.
>
> (SP, 61–62)

11. Warren, "Notes on the Poetry of John Crowe Ransom at His Eightieth Birthday," 342.

The demands of the rhyme seem on occasion to have forced Ransom into an obscure line or two, but the main thrust of the poem is hardly in doubt. Indeed, thematically, "Our Two Worthies" is simply a more sophisticated version of "Sunset."

When Robert Graves wrote to Ransom in August, 1922, expressing enthusiasm over *Poems About God* and requesting more pieces for a new book that would include a selection of the earlier work, the poet chose "a little over half" of the material from his first collection but "had to leave out many as being too theological or too raw (Grace—the sun-stroke thing)" (*SL*, 112). Graves especially wanted "Grace," however, suggesting even that the new volume be called *Grace After Meat*. Following a series of mild protests from Ransom—mainly on aesthetic rather than religious grounds— *Grace After Meat* was published in London in 1924 by Leonard and Virginia Woolf on the recommendation of Graves and Eliot. Graves wrote an introduction to the collection in which he admits that he and Ransom "have had a slight disagreement about the poem 'Grace' which Ransom has grown out of liking on the ground of its hastiness and ugliness, but which I find necessary for the appreciation of the poems of calmer scepticism that follow." He goes on to claim that both Frost and Ransom are "acting spokesmen for those rebellious 'poor whites' (in the political and plutocratic sense) who find the narrow puritanism of their fathers not enough for their needs, and turning sceptic, at first with violence, are beginning to adopt a new religion of nature-worship and toleration of their fellows." [12] Although the latter remark indicates how little Graves understood about American life and even about the poets themselves, it also demonstrates the strongly theological aspect that others saw in Ransom's writings.

From such a perspective, the most famous of Ransom's poems is undoubtedly "Armageddon," which appeared with "Necrological," "Bells for John Whiteside's Daughter," and several other

12. Robert Graves, Introduction to John Crowe Ransom's *Grace After Meat* (London, 1924), 9. In *The Handprinted Books of Leonard and Virginia Woolf at the Hogarth Press, 1917–1932* (Ann Arbor, 1985), Donna E. Rhein notes that Ransom is the "only author of a handprinted book which neither Woolf mentions in writing." Although this omission was probably the result of the Woolfs never having met Ransom, Rhein observes that they "were ill-disposed toward Americans." She adds, "The book [*Grace After Meat*] was still in print in 1939, which might say something for the rest of literary London's opinion of Ransom and American poets between the wars" (55).

poems from the *Fugitive* in his next—and perhaps best—collection, *Chills and Fever*, in 1924. In the conflict between Christ and Antichrist portrayed in the poem, it is the Adversary who appears the more attractive and intelligent figure:

> Antichrist, playing his lissome flute and merry
> As was his wont, debouched upon the plain;
> Then came a swirl of dust, and Christ drew rein,
> Brooding upon his frugal breviary.

Antichrist persuades Christ to don more attractive garments and to discuss theology urbanely with him. When, as a consequence, one of his servants confuses the two, however, Christ is suddenly "discomfited" and "sheds unmannerly his devil's pelf" to engage in battle:

> Christ and his myrmidons, Christ at the head,
> Chanted of death and glory and no complaisance;
> Antichrist and the armies of malfeasance
> Made songs of innocence and no bloodshed.

> The immortal adversary shook his head:
> If now they fought too long, then he would famish;
> And if much blood was shed, why, he was squeamish:
> "These Armageddons weary me much," he said.[13]

At the time this poem was written, Allen Tate criticized it rather cryptically as polemical, its last line a "sermon," suggesting that the Adversary's comment expressed Ransom's own attitude.[14] But, even apart from Tate's comment (which hints, incidentally, that Ransom was not quite sympathetic with the "crisis" mentality of poets such as Tate himself and Eliot), the depiction of Christ as someone who "Chanted of death and glory" hardly seems like a positive recommendation, even if Ransom would later in his prose praise some of the harsher elements of the deity of the Old Testament. What the poem shows most of all, of course, is Ransom's persistent tendency to adopt unorthodox attitudes toward biblical figures and to feel quite unconstrained by the requirements of a scholarly hermeneutics.

"Armageddon" created a problem when it won the annual prize of South Carolina's Poetry Society in 1923, provoking the editor of the *Year Book*, the author of *Porgy and Bess*, to write to an associate:

13. John Crowe Ransom, *Chills and Fever* (New York, 1924), 58–61. The version in *Selected Poems* (1969) has a number of variations, including the last line: "'These Armageddons!' he said; and later bled."
14. Cowan, *The Fugitive Group*, 69.

"Mrs. [Celia] McGowan, aroused by Olive Mathew's report of the nature of Ransom's verse, calls it no less than blasphemy. . . . I hear that a small theological cyclone is brewing against printing 'Armageddon' in the Year Book. . . . The poem *is* radical and scoffing in its tendency, and flippant in its attitude toward figures held sacred by many good men."[15] This could be seen as but the reaction of overpious and unsophisticated readers were it not for the fact that a number of the Fugitives themselves, especially Stanley Johnson and William Frierson, were also taking exception to Ransom's form of unbelief. Tate wrote a poem in 1925, "Causerie," which expresses deep reservations about Ransom's stance in the matter of religion:

> For miracles are faint
> And resurrection is our weakest clause of religion,
> I have known men in my youth who foundered on
> This point of doctrine: John Ransom, boasting hardy
> Entelechies yet botched in the head, lacking grace;
> Warren thirsty in Kentucky, his hair in rain, asleep;
> None so unbaptized as Edmund Wilson the unwearied,
> That sly parody of the devil. They lacked doctrine;
> They waited. I, who watched out the first crisis
> With them, wait.[16]

Here Tate pinpoints once again Ransom's particular difficulty with the Christian message, a difficulty that had been present since the very beginning of his religious questioning: the belief in an afterlife distinct from existence in this present world.

But while poems such as "Vaunting Oak" from *Chills and Fever*, and "Eclogue" and "Persistent Explorer" from Ransom's final collection, *Two Gentlemen in Bonds*, indicate that he was still in some way debating the tensions between "an unbeliever of bitter blood" and more hopeful—if also more innocent—dreamers, still struggling with the sound of water that "spelled nothing" beyond itself, Ransom—unlike Tate and Eliot—was no longer "waiting" or suffering from despair. Indeed, in 1927 he wrote to Tate suggesting that the source of the latter's "unhopefulness" might be that he, like I. A. Richards, was staking "everything on the chance of recovering some cosmological values out of the debris." Ransom claims that his solution is quite different: "The poets are through

15. Quoted in Frank Durham, "The Poetry Society of South Carolina's Turbulent Year: Self-Interest, Atheism, and Jean Toomer," *Southern Humanities Review*, V (Winter, 1971), 77.
16. Allen Tate, *Collected Poems, 1919–1976* (New York, 1977), 14.

with cosmologies and Magical Views. In the place of these vul-
garisms, these obsessions with pure magnitude, they will simply
exhibit the infinite of quality that is in every situation anywhere,
anytime. The poet, again, will simply . . . show . . . how the concept, the poor thin thing, is drowned in the image, how the deter-
minate is drowned in the contingent, and how, ultimately, this
world can neither be understood nor possessed." The only reality,
then, is the concrete world of immediate experience, which requires not so much religious explanation as aesthetic appreciation,
and to which both traditional beliefs and modern science in their
abstractionist tendencies are almost equally opposed: "In the poet's
art we will have to see , if we are willing to look at all, the objec-
tivity of the world; this is a dreadful, an appalling, a religious, and
a humble attitude to which we will come perforce after the con-
ceited Subjectivism into which we have been persuaded by the
practical and the scientific life alike" (SL, 161).

Although Ransom was to write a few significant poems after
1927, the great phase of his creative activity in this field was over by
that date. In a favorable review of Two Gentlemen in Bonds in the
Nation, Tate had remarked, "It may be, of course, that further addi-
tions to the testament complete now with this volume would cry
out redundancy—that Mr. Ransom had overwritten himself."[17]
Ransom said much the same thing to Warren in the mid-1930s,
adding, however, that "if some day I find a new way in, I'll probably start writing [poetry] again." But, given Ransom's strong philosophical bent, a statement made by him in a conversation with
Cleanth Brooks that was published in 1961 seems far more revealing of his state of mind some thirty-four years earlier. Claiming that
his "talent was a modest one," he went on: "I never tried to write
[poetry] and found I couldn't. I just got involved in some of these
theoretical questions—philosophical questions—and they just engage my whole mind." What this comment suggests is that Ransom felt a need to return to a more discursive approach in his intellectual search and that Warren perhaps was not wholly correct
when he remarked that "poetry gave the only way to deal with the
issue."[18]

17. Allen Tate, Review of John Crowe Ransom's Two Gentlemen in Bonds, in Nation, CXXIV (March 30, 1927), 346.
18. Warren, "Notes on the Poetry of John Crowe Ransom at His Eightieth Birthday," 343; Ransom, quoted in Robert Buffington, The Equilibrist: A Study of John
Crowe Ransom's Poems, 1916–1963 (Nashville, 1967), 15.

4

Defining the Problem

In making the transition from *Poems About God* to *Chills and Fever* and *Two Gentlemen in Bonds*, Ransom might be said to have progressed in somewhat Yeatsian fashion from a poetry of "longing and complaint"—or at least of complaint—to one of "insight and knowledge." Nevertheless, as is clear from his many letters to Graves and Tate throughout the 1920s, Ransom was still anxious to work out the details of that knowledge in some more coherent form than poetry itself allowed. By late 1926, therefore, when he had dispatched his final volume of poems to his publisher in New York, he was more than ready for "a season of prose, which," he mused, "may quite envelop my quick spirits" (*SL*, 153).

In particular, Ransom had long been eager to write a book on a certain aesthetic theory that had occupied him since Oxford days. This theory, however, was intimately related to a much wider and more complex set of concerns than such a designation ordinarily suggests, so that the book that eventually emerged at the end of the decade was not about aesthetics proper but rather about religion— "an interlude in my aesthetic interests," he wrote immediately afterwards, "and far from being disconnected with them" (*SL*, 181). Thus, in retrospect, it can be seen that Ransom did not so much undertake three distinct prose enterprises during the 1920s—"The Gothic Principle in the English Literary Tradition," "The Third Moment," and "Giants for Gods"—as experiment with a variety of methods for presenting his central ideas until he found one that was reasonably adequate for his purposes. It was less the case that he had simply abandoned his original intention than that aesthetics and religion were so closely allied in his thinking—even to the extent of overlapping—that, under pressure to get something definite accomplished, he found it more satisfactory to set his thoughts down in a way that was already familiar to him.[1] After all, the religious dimension had, it seemed, preceded the aesthetic—even if later reflection tended to reverse that sequence—for it was the failure of the religious perspective that had made recourse to the aesthetic level necessary. And just as, in the case of the poetry, *Poems About God* had cleared the way for *Chills and Fever,* so too, in the matter of the prose, *God Without Thunder: An Unorthodox Defense of Orthodoxy,* published in 1930, would prepare for *The World's Body,* published in 1938.

It might be wondered, of course, why by this time Ransom was not ready to forget the religious issue altogether and simply get on with examining the aesthetic alternative. The problem was that even if the claims that the various religions made had proved to be unfounded, it was still necessary to account for them as imaginative creations and so to incorporate them as at least a dimension of the aesthetic. Religion, therefore, needed to be opposed to the extent that its propositions were untrue and at the same time to be defended to the degree of its aesthetic veracity. The extent of the problem, however, was not quite clear to Ransom at the beginning of the 1920s, and it was to take him several years to arrive at a coherent solution.

In 1922, then, religion in some form was still of vital concern to Ransom, though he was not in the least interested in reasserting any kind of transcendentalism. The fact that Robert Graves in Oxford was in a similar predicament helped to stimulate their correspondence with each other. Even before Graves wrote the preface to *Grace After Meat,* in which he refers to Ransom and Frost as first "turning sceptic" in their revolt against the narrow puritanism of their fathers, but subsequently "beginning to adopt a new religion of nature-worship and toleration of their fellows," he had published in *The Feather Bed,* in 1923, an introductory letter addressed to Ransom in which he gives a curious account of the development of the idea of God: from his reading of the Old and New Testaments, he had concluded that the Jewish idea of God had "three stages at least," progressing from the God created by animal instincts, to the God of social order that tries to repress the former deity, and, finally, to Lucifer, the Morning Star, "the hope of even-

---

1. Vanderbilt's Chancellor Kirkland had been inquiring from time to time about the progress of Ransom's book (*SL,* 178–79).

tual adjustment between ancient habits and present needs."[2] The general thrust of *Poems About God* had most likely prompted Graves to write this introductory letter, and some of Graves's unusual ideas would in turn be reflected in Ransom's *God Without Thunder* seven years later.

On July 4, 1924, in the midst of this discussion and in response to reading *Mock Beggar Hall*, a volume of "barely versified philosophical speculations" that Graves had produced in collaboration with an Indian student of philosophy, Basanta Mallik, Ransom wrote commending Graves for having "a content, a philosophy, a system of ideas that you can hold with passion." Ransom—who describes himself as "prepared to go to the absolute limit in accepting everything that you say"—continues with an explanation of why he himself needs to follow this example: "I have been feeling rather the lack of a positive in my own work; feeling, that is, that I was only partially expressing myself, and along satirical and negative lines mostly when I was sure that I was capable of a doctrine, a dogma more or less inspired, anything to give the heathen after trying to destroy their feeble superstitions. . . . I am sure that a certain stage of poetics is now past for me, and there'll be a Religion in whatever I put forth next" (*SL*, 138).

But if Ransom's rather bleak message in his poems had not been sufficient to sustain his readers, what possible kind of "Religion" could a convinced skeptic like him propose? Such a question must have been very much on his mind at the time because just two days later he again wrote to Graves about the same book. In his letter Ransom states that he finds himself in agreement with Graves concerning the limitations of the "occidental" mind (a favorite expression), the utmost reach of which is to solve the conflict between different religious beliefs "by faith and the leap-in-the-dark which is the Western view of Christianity—'I acted as my Savior approves action'"—but which is for "babes rather than philosophers." Graves, rightly, wants "perfect understanding" in this area. But then Ransom (no longer, apparently, willing "to go to the absolute limit in accepting everything" that Graves says) goes on to criticize him for subsequently departing from this requirement and apparently resorting to providence to settle the conflict. "The ques-

2. Robert Graves, *The Feather Bed* (London, 1923), 3. A detailed summary of the letter is available in Michael Kirkham's *The Poetry of Robert Graves* (New York, 1969), 73–74.

tion will be raised," he writes, "as to what after all is the nature of your solution; particularly, how your solution differs from that of the Christian religion, and whether it does not approach neo-Hegelian absolutism which is the western equivalent of orientalism but which is in practice vanity and annihilation" (SL, 141). This is the kind of comment that an anti-idealist such as Ransom might well have made in regard to Bradley's philosophy also, and one that indicates his strong reluctance to seek his desired "Religion" in the obscurities of an alternative Eastern mysticism. Earlier he had written Graves that he had "never however been able to follow their [Indian] dialectic which is so annihilating to all the edge, point, shape, and individuality of Anglo-Saxon concepts—I'm racially incapable of doing a Buddha" (SL, 127). But neither, according to Ransom in the present letter, will a general skepticism do, for while it "destroys dogma and faces truth gladly, and cannot be unprofitable," in the end it is negative. Then, tending as usual to read his own preoccupations into Graves's work, or at least trying to make it conform to them, he concludes with an echo of his missive of two days previously: "Your next step will be a religion of some kind; I feel that your position still stops short" (SL, 141).

In gradually becoming aware that he would have to negotiate between skepticism and credulity, and in attempting to cope with "the lack of a positive" in his own work, Ransom was shifting slightly from a concern with the truth or falsehood of religious claims to speculation on their importance for the well-being of the imagination. In other words, his earlier offense had become a defense, though only for a time and in a manner that would have quite disconcerted an informed orthodox believer. This shift—provoked in part, certainly, by the debate then raging over the Scopes monkey trial, which had tended rather naïvely to exalt the scientific at the expense of the religious and imaginative—is evident again in another letter to Graves in December, 1925, in which he outlines a project ("The Gothic Principle in the English Literary Tradition") for a Guggenheim Fellowship that he hopes to use at Oxford.[3] Beginning with a chapter on the nature of genius and then one on Shakespeare, he will have

3. Ransom was not in any way involved with the trial that took place in Dayton, Tennessee, in 1925. Nevertheless, he refused his university's call to condemn publicly the obscurantism of the antievolutionists because he felt that they, however ignorantly and inadequately, stood for the values of the imagination over those of an abstract science insensitive to such considerations.

a very fine chapter, I think, on Religion and Gothic, in which I show that all religions that are vital are a folk product first, and contain sensational and obscene features in plenty: but get themselves taken up by the higher critics, theologians, and Liberals, who try to emasculate them of their Gothic quality—whereas they cannot survive this process if they are to stay the religions of the whole society. And a chapter on science as anti-Gothic, which makes this point: The scientists are exactly like Plato. . . . The whole interest of science is to classify and generalize, and it has no patience with human personality or even the stubborn familiar thinghood of things; and art and religion between them save this sense of existence to the people. (*SL*, 148)

Whatever kind of religion Ransom was trying to defend, it was clearly a good deal less orthodox than that which even his liberal-minded ministerial father was preaching at the time.

Ransom failed to win the Guggenheim, and it was 1926 before he was granted a leave of absence from Vanderbilt to undertake his ambitious project. In the meantime, this had been changed from "The Gothic Principle in the English Literary Tradition" to a more philosophically oriented analysis titled simply "The Third Moment" but more accurately described years later as "a kind of Prolegomena to Any Future Poetic" (*WB*, vii). The surviving outline of the epistemological system that Ransom hoped to offer (which shows influences from much of the philosophical reading he had been doing since his Oxford days) makes it plain that the project was an attempt at both founding and justifying his own claims for the values of poetry and the imagination as against those of science.

The first moment of Ransom's system is that in which a familiar experience takes place, "unreflective, concrete, and singular." The second is characterized by the formation of concepts through the process of abstracting from what originally occurred. But a process of *subtracting* is taking place also, for the concepts fail to include all the richness and variety of the first moment. Hence the nonconceptualized, the nonuseful—and Ransom quite clearly equates the useful with the scientific—is temporarily relegated to Bergson's realm of Pure Memory or to the Freudian unconscious. It is the consequent awareness that something is missing that provokes the advance to the third and final moment, in which concrete image and abstract concept from the first two stages are united so that there is "a sort of practicable reconciliation of the two worlds." There is, however, a hierarchy within this third moment, from lowest to highest: dreams ("compensatory regressions not intended"), fancies ("*consent* is present"), religion ("where we are almost conscious of the significance of the state"), morals ("which ignor[e] cognition and calculation"), and art ("attended with pretty complete purpose and sophistication"). Poetry—and, Ransom ought to have added, only poetry that conforms to the definitions he would subsequently give for that art—dwells in the third moment because it is "always the exhibit of Opposition and at the same time Reconciliation between the Conceptual or Formal and the Individual or Concrete" (*SL*, 155–57).

There is no need to go into some of the difficulties suggested by such an account—Ransom himself was all too aware that its elaboration would be quite problematic—except to observe that religion is subordinated to art as a mode of "almost" to one of "complete" consciousness. It would seem (though this is not at all clear) that religion is not "complete" because of its frequently Platonizing tendencies, its insistence on dogma rather than on ritual, which preclude it from adequate realization of its proper aesthetic element. In any case, Ransom was to hold to the general outline of this sequence of moments throughout his life, and it was on this basis that, for example, more than thirty years later he would criticize the report of Wordsworth's religious intuitions as given in several of that writer's most famous poems.

Ransom did not see himself as indulging in the kind of aesthetic escapism that had begun with the Romantics and that is especially associated with late nineteenth-century English literature, appearing in certain works of Walter Pater and W. B. Yeats, for example. Rather, in his view, the aesthetic experience alone gives access to reality in all its wonder *and* terror, so that in truth it is abstractionist and falsely consoling religion and science that should most accurately be accused of escapist tendencies:

> My view is that we must, as critics, not only define the fictions of science for what they are, but also the fictions of philosophy. Philosophy of the usual or "constructive" sort, and not of the Kantian or critical sort, is an attempt to formulate in a more sophisticated way, but still, to formulate, the reality which science has quite obviously failed to grasp. So are religious systems. Their formulas must be questioned. . . . The State, the Soul, God, the World, the Cosmos (with a capital)—these are types of the scientific fiction put together by reason and quite exceeding the senses: Supersensibles. They have in this condition no aesthetic quality, no reality.   (*SL*, 162)

Ransom's conclusion, therefore, which he thinks is supported by his reading of the American New Realist philosophers (specifically R. B. Perry and E. G. Spaulding), who were carrying on the tradition of James, Bergson, and Russell, is that "what we require is to return simply to the senses" and that "it is quite a quaint idea that we are to find this world out there somewhere transcending sense" (*SL*, 162–63). Thus, in contrast with Tate, who was still trying to create a poetry that was based on an outworn mythology, or "in a dark despair" because such a mythology did not currently exist, Ransom considered himself to be more radical, to the extent even of throwing over all cosmologies and "quantitative Infinities" to become (at least within the license allowed by epistolary rhetoric) "a desperate Positivist, Nominalist, Philistine, Sensationalist, and Sceptic" (*SL*, 165).

Furthermore, though Ransom's lengthier commentaries on Eliot would not begin to appear for another ten years, the author of *The Waste Land* is always in the background to what Ransom finds most objectionable in his friend Tate's (once self-described as Eliot's "distant disciple") social and religious attitudes; it was in fact Tate's angry response to Ransom's review of Eliot's poem in 1923 that led shortly afterwards to the only serious crisis in their long friendship.[4] So, in 1927, in the months in which Eliot was preparing to pass through the doors of Finstock Church in Oxfordshire as an Anglican convert, Ransom was writing to Tate on the same topic in an entirely different vein:

> And as for religion, we observe the continuous degeneration of every faith. By a universal & melancholy law of its nature, apparently. In this way: Religion begins pure; it is—cf. Schleiermacher—our sense of impotence before a greater [Power?] than we, our humble confession of impotence, our philosophy of Objectivity; and then very soon it becomes a desperate frightened effort to *placate* this Objectivity and make it amenable after all; whether you call it at this stage magic or whether you call it Faith in God or whether even you call it a philosophical embrace of the Absolute. Its end becomes the practical after all: "What I could not gain by Science & Will I can gain by insight and renunciation—I win after all." . . . The inevitable tendency of religion is to slide downhill.

Religion can be saved only if its aesthetic feature can adopt new forms suited to the age. But Ransom then adds the key statement:

4. Young, *Gentleman in a Dustcoat*, 150–55.

"Actually—for you and me and the elite whom I know—art is the true religion and no other is needed" (SL, 167–68). Tate, always tending toward the kind of religious orthodoxy that Eliot was just then embracing, would hardly have agreed.

In February, 1928, on Tate's recommendation, Ransom sent a chapter (with the rather Wittgensteinian title "Pictures and Things") from "The Third Moment" to Eliot at the Criterion. This was prefaced with the self-defeating remark that "this sort of thing is far too stiff and formidable for our American periodicals" (SL, 177). There is no record of Eliot's reply, and the chapter was never published separately as an essay, but the dissatisfaction with the abstract nature of his enterprise that comes across even in his own brief letter was to prompt Ransom a year later to abandon his completed manuscript for yet another new work, titled this time "Giants for Gods." Still, his 1929 essay "Classical and Romantic," which he referred to as a "condensation" of some of his arguments from "The Third Moment," clearly indicates how closely that epistemological project foreshadowed his next undertaking (SE, 35–44; SL, 179).

On July 4, 1929, five years to the day from when he had written Graves that "there'll be a Religion in whatever I put forth next," Ransom wrote Tate that he had been working on a "hot & hasty book on religion" that was at least "sincere." Some idea of the book's contents is given in the following extract from the letter:

> It is just as you say: Religion is fundamental and prior to intelligent (or human) conduct on any plane. . . . It is our only guarantee of security and—an item that seems to me to carry a good deal of persuasive power—the enjoyment of life. The fear of the Lord is the beginning of wisdom; a big beginning, but only a beginning of which the end is the love of the Lord. Substitute nature for the Lord and he won't feel aggrieved. The Jews knew all about that in their Old Testament; the New Testament was a temptation which the soft-headed Western World couldn't resist; in the N.T. it seems (to the soft-headed W.W.) that the love of the Lord is the beginning of wisdom, and it's the kind of love . . . a scientist bears to the gentle, tractable elements in his test-tubes, which so gladly yield him of their secrets, and work for him. The N.T. has been a failure & a backset as a religious myth; not its own fault, as I think, but nevertheless a failure; it's hurt us.

Graves's ideas of 1923 (though Ransom himself had long been thinking in similar terms) are reflected in the further remark that many myth systems have been concerned with giants "who were not Gods but only demi-Gods, yet *thought* they were Gods and be-

haved accordingly. Prometheus, for example . . . Satan is the Hebrew Prometheus and so conceived in Milton's P[aradise] L[ost]—
he is *Lucifer*. . . . But then *Jesus is Lucifer* again" (*SL*, 180–81).
Ransom had finally chosen to write about religion—his own peculiar version in which one can "substitute nature for the Lord" and
"*Jesus is Lucifer*"—rather than about aesthetics as such because he
believed religion represented the most widely disseminated form
of the aesthetic experience, though he also thought that it was fast
losing this dimension. Religion had an audience greater than that
which existed for poetry, and so by saving it from its own worst
instincts one might also save the poetic imagination from disap-
pearance, thus enabling human beings to face the full truth of their
mortal condition.

"Giants for Gods," then, written in a nine-week flurry of activity
in 1929, and retitled and published as *God Without Thunder*, retains
several of the ideas from Ransom's discarded manuscript on aesthetics as well as from his aborted study of the Gothic element in
literature. It shows that he was quite conversant with contemporary criticisms of scientific knowledge and offers a number of extended discussions of philosophical and scientific concepts. Although Louise Cowan is surely exaggerating when she claims that
"ideas throughout its pages anticipate Carl Jung, Mircea Eliade,
Eric Voegelin, Susanne Langer, Philip Wheelwright, and other
writers treating the topics of myth, symbol, and culture," the book
belongs in a general way to the tradition of Alfred North Whitehead's *Science and the Modern World* and similar works by Bertrand
Russell and Arthur Eddington rather than to that of theological po-
lemics as such.[5] Ransom had at last committed his religious ideas to
print, had given the problem a definition, so that it would no
longer be necessary simply to use his poetry to speculate about
what he thought concerning the nature and possibility of religious
belief. He was now, however, in pursuit of a very strange God
indeed.

5. Louise Cowan, *The Southern Critics* (Dallas, 1971), 24.

5

Necessary Myths

"That is a peculiar book for me to write," Ransom remarked to Robert Penn Warren in 1930 shortly after the publication of *God Without Thunder*, "but I wanted to pursue the logic of the subject." It was "peculiar," he added, because "I have a strong streak of *skepticism* in my make-up." Nevertheless, he had set himself the task of working out the best logical case possible for religion so that he could then contemplate it.[1] In spite of this emphasis on logic, however (or maybe, in a deeper sense, because of it), the book has a number of serious—one is tempted to say thundering—inconsistencies. The very haste with which *God Without Thunder* was finally written served to make it a more straightforward and honest book than a longer and more considered reflection might have advised. Here, indeed, Ransom contemplates out loud, and for himself as much as for anyone else.

Whatever the work's local confusions and contradictions, its main emphasis is never in doubt. Wayne A. Knoll, a Jesuit theologian, has summed up its theme quite neatly: "Since God does not exist, and since man needs myth for psychological and practical reasons, Ransom affirms the advantage of and necessity for the Supreme Myth, that figment of the mind which corresponds to all that does exist . . . or all in the world that is both perceptible and ineffable because of the richness of matter." Although this account may be excessively critical of the precise extent of Ransom's theistic beliefs, it does point clearly to the strange nature of his religious defense. "Mr. Ransom's book," a contemporary reviewer wrote,

---

1. Robert Penn Warren to author, May 5, 1985. This is an elaboration of a statement made in Warren, "Notes on the Poetry of John Crowe Ransom at His Eightieth Birthday," 325.

"far from being a defense of orthodoxy, is a repudiation of the Christian religion, in its doctrinal and practical aspects."[2]

However that may be, Ransom dedicated *God Without Thunder* to his father and prefaced it with a letter to Sidney Mttron Hirsch, the host to the Fugitives who was most interested in the occult and in Eastern religions and whose views on the subject Ransom had earlier so much enjoyed deflating. The letter employs a strategy very similar to that used in the introduction to *Poems About God* in that Ransom is again disingenuously attempting to dissociate himself from the unorthodoxy of what follows. In the letter Ransom explains that though he himself is "the son of a theologian, and the grandson of another one . . . the gift did not come down to me" (ix). He is writing therefore as a layman for the laity, and so he continues:

> I have some confidence that you will think my view of religion to be the true and orthodox one. But my policy of frankly analyzing the religious experience is certainly not so orthodox, and it is not unlikely that you will question its expediency. It is as if I had said here of the sacred objects and the supernaturalisms of the faith: Behold these myths! Then I have defined the myths, in the cold and not very fastidious terms of an Occidental logic. That has never been the way, I understand very well, of the true priests. But it is a policy which is at least permitted to me, and which is at the moment, I judge, the most appropriate one.

Since the recent attack by scientists and philosophers on myths of every kind has, according to Ransom, led to an increased poverty of mind, he is undertaking to explain in "simple untechnical monosyllables" the function of myths in human civilization (ix–x).

God Without Thunder, then, is essentially about the importance of the mythic imagination for society at large. The division of the chapters is not absolutely clear, and there are a number of repetitions within and between sections. In general, however, the first and longest part of the book explains—following an initial criticism of contemporary religion for its alliance with science—why myths are necessary and how they function; the second and third parts then offer detailed elaborations of two specific arguments made only briefly in the first part, namely, that science, like religion, is

---

2. Wayne A. Knoll, "Ransom as Religionist," *Mississippi Quarterly,* XXX (Winter, 1976–77), 132; William S. Knickerbocker, Review of Ransom's *God Without Thunder,* in *Sewanee Review,* XXXIX (Winter, 1931), 111.

based on undemonstrable metaphysical principles and that a god worthy of intelligent worship should be constituted in a particular way; and, finally, the short epilogue aims at providing a program of action.

Ransom begins with an attack on various contemporary efforts at reaching a compromise between science and religion, an attack that echoes remarks made in his letters to Tate of the late 1920s. Such an adaptation of orthodoxy to modern science is "fundamentally irreligious, or secular, both in its doctrines and in its works" (5). *Orthodoxy* he defines as the religion of the Eastern, or Orthodox, church, less so of the Roman and Anglican churches, even less so again of the nonconformists, eventually tapering off "towards the vanishing point, by varying degrees which I could not define, into Unitarianism"—an observation that is certainly interesting in the light of Ransom's subsequent identification with that body (4–5).

What is actually happening in the religious sphere? The stern and inscrutable God of the Old Testament is being replaced by an amiable and understandable God: "We wanted a God who wouldn't hurt us; who would let us understand him; who would agree to scrap all the wicked thunderbolts in his armament. And this is just the God that has developed popularly out of the Christ of the New Testament: the embodiment mostly of the principle of social benevolence and of physical welfare" (5). Ransom's objection here, obviously, is not to the unbelievers but rather to those believers who would pretend that the world is other than it really is: a harsh and difficult place. The doctrine to which he is opposed is "that God as the ruler of the universe governs it in such a manner as to make it accommodate itself to the welfare of man. The earth is for man's abode; and God 'developed' it; this phrase suggests that his instrument was an evolutionary or scientific process. Thus God is a scientist; the universe is his workshop; but among his productions he has produced man, and all the other productions are for man's benefit" (16).

It is the Protestant churches, whose rise coincides with that of modern science, that are responsible for this viewpoint, while the Roman Catholic church continues to oppose the secularization of God (28). God is now equated with nature, and the attempt is to study and possess him and to subject him to law. Ransom quotes R. A. Millikan, a Nobel Laureate in physics, as the most influential purveyor of the new religion. According to Millikan, "The idea that

God, or Nature, or the Universe . . . is not a being of caprice and whim" but instead rules through law in a universe of consistency and orderliness, "has *made* modern science, and it is unquestionably the foundation of modern civilization" (31). To counteract this view, Ransom makes the first of many highly unorthodox assertions: far from being benign, God is in fact the author of evil as well as of good. He writes:

> The Jews [of the Old Testament] were scarcely prepared to say, with the moderns, that they possessed a God whose simple function was to promote their good. They found too much realistic testimony to the contrary. The God who governed their universe was a spirit so inscrutable, so contingent, so mysterious, that his works could never be fully accounted for, and among these works of his will were evidently works that brought suffering upon human beings. To put this into words of one and two syllables: *God is the author of evil as well as good, and one can never be sure which of the two is coming next.* (39–40)

One of the arguments that Ransom uses to justify this assertion (without regard to scholarship on the subject or, indeed, to logic) is that there are two biblical accounts of King David's census of Israel: in the first, Satan moves David to number the people of Israel, while in the second, Jehovah causes David to take the census (41–42). Thus Satan, or evil, is identified with God.

Ransom's belief that God is the author of evil is not merely based on textual evidence; rather, he conceives that the world is made up irremediably of both good and evil and that whatever being made it must contain both qualities. Ransom distinguishes his attitude on this point from that of Bertrand Russell. Russell is as realistic about the world's indifference and inhumanity as he himself is but refuses as a consequence to worship an immoral God. Ransom, however, sees an inappropriate defiance in this attitude; for him, it is better to adapt one's mind to reality, to a universe that is "beyond good and evil." His religion, he explains, "enlarges the God it worships, upon finding that the God That Is will not reduce to the God That Is Good" (49).

Ransom is even willing to alter the biblical text to suit his own conception of the divinity. He is pleased, for example, when Job accepts the inscrutability of God's will, but then declares: "I exercise my privilege again, and pass over as an unworthy anti-climax the epilogue in which God, who has thus humbled the pride of Job, relieves his sufferings and gives him twice as much of worldly prosperity as he has had before. This is somebody's 'happy ending' which spoils a tragedy" (50–51). Although the conclusion to the story of Job is indeed one of the texts that is in dispute among biblical scholars, it is clear that here Ransom is prepared to make his own independent judgment with or without their support.

Having tackled the emasculation of religion that has taken place even in the churches themselves, Ransom passes on to a more general defense of his position. It is here that his own unorthodoxy is most strikingly revealed, especially coming so soon after his attack on others whose views in many important respects can be seen to resemble his. He declares quite openly his "faith": "I believe that religious myths, including those of the Bible, are unhistorical and unscientific, precisely as our gallant historians and higher critics have recently discovered; but that their unhistorical and unscientific character is not their vice but their excellence, and that it certainly was their intent" (55).

It takes Ransom several pages to explain this paradoxical conclusion. His basic argument, however, is that whereas science aims at a general knowledge of regularities in nature, the myth of an object "is its proper name, private, unique, untranslatable, overflowing, of a demonic energy that cannot be reduced to the poverty of the class-concept." Hence, in order to know the world in its particularity, myth is necessary. In a similar way, particular events in history require their respective myths in order to be fully apprehended: "The myth of an event is a story, which invests the natural with a supernatural background, and with a more-than-historical history." The point, then, is that, as Ransom claims in one of the numerous italicized sentences that punctuate his narrative, *"myth resorts to the supernatural in order to represent the fullness of the natural"* (65). The mythmaker is intent upon stinging us into awareness of the individual image in much the same way that poets "are constantly creating little local myths, in their rebellion against the destructive terms of a routine presentation" (66). Thus there are two reasons why the myth of God has been invented: first, that man needs a being to represent the indefiniteness of time and space; second, that since the cosmos is not simply "the sum of its constants," it requires a God to symbolize its individuality. *"The myth is not descriptive, it is prescriptive"* (68).

But religion is neither alone nor unusual in needing prescriptive myths, for science too, as Ransom now seeks to show rather briefly (he will develop the point in more detail in the next part), also requires them. "There are supernatural assumptions which science has to make right from the beginning, and as long as it undertakes to be science" (72). The scientist must believe, for example, in the principle of causality, a principle that is not in itself demonstrable and so must be considered metaphysical. Other examples of metaphysical entities that one can legislate into being include substances, minds, and selves—none of which are demonstrable but all of which one must believe in in order to undertake a satisfactory science. "A [metaphysical] Principle insisted on, stuck to, meant, developed in detail, defined, professed, becomes a God," declares Ransom (82). He continues:

> The Gods who have been legislated into official existence by the will of the whole society are defined in myths which tell what they are like; how they have performed in the physical universe and in human history; what sorts of conduct they require from their subjects, the members of the community. The sanctity, majesty, divinity, taboo, with which they are invested, are to represent in the most binding way possible the power and determination of the social will that lies behind them. Their commandments are the oldest and most fundamental prescriptions which society has imposed upon itself. Under the picturesque terms of the myth this ancient body of legislation comes down to us translated into Divine Revelation, and this old and continuing will of society becomes Divine Authority.   (84)

Far from being a traditional religious view, Ransom's perspective here is very much akin to those of early twentieth-century anthropologists or to that of Frazer's *Golden Bough*.

It is quite in keeping with this independent approach that Ransom goes on to specify some of the characteristics that this God myth is required to possess. It should, for example, be concrete—that is, be stern as well as benevolent—for "the God who survives must embody our fullest idea of the universe" (87). Such is the case, Ransom thinks, with the God who is affirmed in the Apostles' Creed. A more disconcerting requirement, perhaps, is that the myth must suit man "racially and culturally." Occidentals, for example, cannot have a rain god or even a god who is too obviously Jewish. Finally, such a myth must be socially acceptable and receive social expression (89).

A problem arises, however, when—as happens all too often—unsophisticated believers, forgetting that man himself has created the myth of God, attempt to change the sequence of nature by invoking the power of the deity through prayer and sacrifice. "But in this sense prayer is vain . . . and vain is every form of rite in the Christian communion, early or late. The idea of ritual as an effective influence upon the natural order of events is entertained today as it has always been, and it still indicates a very feeble talent for epistemology, for the analysis of the terms of his knowledge, on the part of the man who entertains it. He is scarcely informed of the sense and intention with which the myth-maker created the God" (94). There is no point, obviously, in praying to a mere term that one has invented oneself.

The overall religious view that Ransom is recommending is described by him as "Fundamentalist." According to his unique—not to say astonishing—definition, the Fundamentalist begins as a philosopher, establishing principles, and then passes on to the mythical forms of these principles, namely God; finally, he picks out *"of all the myths a particular one to profess and to keep"* (95). But because the believer has done the choosing himself, he cannot be expected to keep constantly reminding himself that what he believes in is myth, not fact: "The Fundamentalist, to borrow Kant's phrase again, has *legislated* his God into being, not found him somewhere, and if he means business he will stand by his own legislation. He makes himself a little bit absurd if he continues to suspect it, to demand its credentials, and to force himself to go each time through the agonies of his original decision" (98). Ransom's Fundamentalist, therefore, does not pray for privileged treatment from God; instead, his prayer "reconciles him to his impending defeat" in a universe that is indifferent to his very existence (100–101).

It need hardly be stressed that Ransom's maneuvering here has nothing whatsoever to do with a defense of the southern Fundamentalist churches, for his theology is blatantly agnostic if not downright atheistic. This fact becomes even more evident when Ransom goes on to discuss the two great opponents of the grimly realistic view of the world that he has just presented: Satan and Christ. Satan, as the Garden of Eden myth clearly shows, inspired man to pursue knowledge and hence to believe in that fanatical doctrine of progress that now makes him prey more and more on nature and in consequence become increasingly alienated from it. Centuries later, John Milton understood the fatal significance of this outcome when he finally repudiated his heroic but dangerous Lucifer of *Paradise Lost* because his own "realistic observations of life" had convinced him that tragedy, not progress, was the inevitable lot of man (134).

Christ too, if not in his own person, then in the statements of his followers, has been incepted into the party of those unwilling to face the harsh reality of this world. "A subordinate figure in the early Christian Godhead," notes Ransom, Christ has now become, "or at least he is rapidly becoming, the whole Godhead." Thus "by an exquisite irony the disciples of Christ have disobeyed his admonitions, forgotten his limits, and made him assume the throne after all—where he sits now quite incompetent to rule over the dominions of another. In this false position he cannot do them much good. They are simply doomed to disappointment" (140–41). Christ's doctrine of heaven and hell—which was more Platonic than derived from the Old Testament—has been replaced by a belief in heaven only, though Ransom suggests that either belief "relies upon a hope which realism is powerless to support" (151).

When Ransom sums up his position, however, he offers a partial compromise between the opposing factions: "Religion is the system of myths which gives a working definition to the relation of man to nature. It always has to join together in some fashion two quite different views of this relation. The first is that of nature as usable and intelligible for man: nature as a humane order, devoted to man's welfare, created by a benevolent God for the purpose of man's service. The second is that of nature as unintelligible and contingent, and therefore alien and unusable for man: nature as an order that is not the humane or ethical order" (156). Occidentals (and the New Testament) favor the first view, Orientals (and the Old Testament) the second. Ransom prefers some middle course between the two, for one is too benign, the other too cruel. But most significant is that religion is considered to be nothing more than "the system of myths which gives a working definition to the relation of man to nature."

Ransom's task in Part Two of God Without Thunder is to develop some of the philosophical concepts to which he merely alluded in the first part; that is, he proposes to examine in more detail the intellectual credentials of science and to show that the adversary of religion and poetry has indeed its own intractable problems. By way of introduction, he presents his strongest objection to the technology that science—and he does not distinguish very clearly between the two fields—eventually produces: it blinds man to his true situation in the world. "The toys which science showers upon us are therefore amusements just a little more than innocent; for they flatter us and quiet our apprehension: they are anodynes. The speeding driver in the car cannot afford to observe the infinite variety of nature, he must confirm his sense of power. He is deliberately practicing a technique of anesthesia" (174). According to Ransom, man constantly lowers his perception of what happiness consists in so that it may be satisfied by the mechanical products of the scientific intelligence, while he also—quite hopelessly—attempts to escape from the reality of a life circumscribed by the certainty of death and disease.

When Ransom applies himself to the task in hand, though he repeats and extends some of the criticisms of science that had been made widely familiar by contemporary philosophers (or philosophical scientists) such as Russell, Eddington, J. S. Haldane, and Whitehead, the names to which he refers most frequently are those of Hume, Kant, and Bergson (187, 206). Hume, for example, pointed out that by accepting the nonempirical concept of causality scientists "very generally confused their facts and their fictions" (210). According to Ransom, what is really significant about Hume, however, is that by being so skeptical he upset those scientists of his own day who had previously made disparaging remarks about the religious establishment: "Their skepticism was a damaging one to apply against religionists who said they saw and heard and felt their God. . . . But then came David Hume. . . . He did not hunt down the simple religionists, he found his game among the enlightened scientists. They were thinking or imagining their objects, often enough, which could never be demonstrated or placed on the level of actual reality. Hume's delicious pastime was to hoist the engineer with his own petard" (221). Here, of course, Ransom conveniently ignores this philosopher's equally troublesome views on the religious phenomenon.

Nonetheless, Hume honestly admitted that he too (like the scientists) found himself constrained to posit the nonempirical concepts of substance and person in order to give focus to the bundles of disparate experiences of which each individual is composed. Ransom thinks that it is justifiable to extend this positing to include concepts such as evolution, life, élan vital, and the State, none of which can be seen or felt. Moreover, all of them, he argues rather unconvincingly, point to a (divine) Person as their source: "The person may not be so called, he may go disguised as a Principle, or Guiding Force, or Impersonal Intelligence: but these explanations are dodges: look hard and they stand for a person." His conclusion is that much of science, like religion, "is busy with exhibiting spirits of one kind or another" (214).

Kant brought about a major change in Hume's philosophy by providing it with sorely needed underpinnings. While he allowed that "the causes, the forces, the powers, and all their kind, which bulked large in their scientific importance, were only fictions," he added, "They are necessary fictions, which it is according to the constitution of our minds to compose." According to Ransom, "Kant humanized, regularized, and classified—and in that sense justified—the fictions. If all men were obliged to think in some manner of A as the cause of B, then the proposition that A was the cause of B had a universality: it was valid for the mind everywhere" (215–16). Presumably the same might be said on behalf of the Person that Ransom had argued for earlier.

But whereas Kant solved Hume's problem that "science tells more than the truth," Bergson helped show that "science tells less than the truth [of naked experience]." He pointed out the limitations of scientific abstraction, which fails to come to terms with the particular, and also demonstrated that nature is indeterminate and that consciousness is free. However, Bergson occupied himself with "defending the particularity of living organisms, and of states of mind" and neglected inanimate objects. But these too, according to Ransom, "being particular," are of "inexhaustible qualitative variety" and have a "concrete energy" that "will never submit to determination" (218–19).

Finally in this part, Ransom devotes a chapter to attacking the proposition that everything—including the other sciences—can be reduced to physics alone. Such astute theorists of science as Eddington and Russell have been misled by this idea and so are all the more valuable as exhibits "of what the powerful temptations of science will do to even a very critical mind" (223). Ransom argues in considerable detail that Eddington's "atomic" table (composed mainly of empty space) and Russell's "geographical machine" (which potentially could predict all events in history) are mere fictions that in the end require concrete, particular embodiments. What this part does, then, is to show that science is ultimately dependent on metaphysical principles similar to those that religion requires and that, moreover, in itself it is insufficient to account for the concrete variety either of the inanimate objects or of the life around us.

The awkward title of Part Three of Ransom's book—"Ghosts: Including the Holy"—is an indication of the idiosyncrasy of much of its content. Building on the preceding claims, Ransom now attempts to offer a more systematic argument (or series of arguments) for the concrete God that he presented briefly in the first section—even going so far at one point as to explain why and how the Greek Orthodox church is indeed the most truly orthodox of all the denominations. He declares that the principles, gods, and fictions that are necessarily presumed in the scientific enterprise can also be called "ghosts," a term he chooses because of its connotations of mysteriousness and unreality. He would wish to call the famous scientific ether a ghost in this sense because it was a necessary postulate in the totality of a complex theory, even though there was no measurable evidence of its actual existence (252). Supersensible objects—England, the Roman Catholic church, the twentieth century—would also qualify for this category. But precisely because these are categorical ghosts, they fail to embrace the concreteness of the individual object. Ransom calls the latter—following a somewhat strained argument about the respective capacities of mathematical surds and the act of personification to suggest the concepts of infinitude and richness—a demon or concrete ghost. *Demon* he derives from the Greek *daimon*, which "stood for the secret, or ineffable, or transcendental individuality of some individual and private person"—such as Socrates (287). These are "very local ghosts, but they have variety. . . . They gratify that impulse of the mind, perhaps not so common an impulse with us as the religious impulse, to contemplate for its own sake the object as a concrete object, or as an inexhaustible complex of attributes. Hence the demon or concrete ghost. The demon is inscrutable, various, baffling, and evil as well as good" (301).

When Ransom proceeds to apply these distinctions to the matter of God, he makes the general point that traditionally God has been conceived of as a metaphysical entity and that this conception can be justified by science in the sense that it too needs metaphysical foundations, but at the same time, this is an inadequate conception of God since it leaves him without concrete embodiment. Hence it is necessary to find some way of uniting the concept of God as categorical ghost with that of him as demonic, or concrete, ghost. Ransom does precisely this in what, without apparent self-consciousness, he calls "a stroke of genius":

> But a great stroke is possible here. If the Universal Ghost has the theological dimensions but not the esthetic variety, and if the Concrete Ghost has the variety but not the dimensions. . . . Why not invest the Logos with a hypothetical demonism, or, if you will, invest the Demon with a hypothetical universality, and create the Hypothesis of all Hypotheses, or the Ghost of Ghosts? *This great Ghost will be the Logos of all the Demons, or the Demon of all the Logoi.* He will be a Person in both the senses of a person: in his freedom and in his magnitude. He will be, I am convinced, that formidable being to which the ladder of Hegel led: *the Concrete Universal.*
> This is evidently a stroke of genius. It obviates at once that weakness which has so often proved fatal to religions: the unearthly and impracticable purity of their God. It also removes the limitation which has so often crippled art: the localism or point-like isolation of the esthetic object. It enables our act of worship to partake of the substantiality of esthetic experience. And it enables our arts to rise to the dignity of worship.   (301–302)

Ransom goes on immediately to emphasize that subsequent Hegelians have not been faithful to this "Concrete Universal" concept of God (having broken the fragile synthesis by opting for universality over concreteness) and that this concept is certainly not embodied in the Christ of the New Testament or in the Holy Ghost when conceived of as a comforter of man's distress. But then Ransom explains what the true nature of the Holy Ghost is as he understands it:

> Representing as he does the demonic qualifications, the Holy Ghost was an appropriate addition to the Godhead at a critical time. The inscrutable and awful God of the Jews . . . was being reduced to a Father, who had acknowledged man as his son and heir, and upon whose goodness man was quite ready to presume. But the rational and humane essence which he had imparted through the act of paternity . . . had not exhausted his nature, nor defined the entire process by which he governed his universe. There was also an essence, an exceedingly energetic one, which was irrational and contingent, for all that human reason could do to compass it, and either indifferent or cruel, for all that it seemed to sympathize with human desires. So the Holy Ghost was the ghost who came to bear witness of God in his fullness.   (313)

Whatever "comfort" this Holy Ghost might have brought with him was that "of being possessed with the Spirit of Truth: the comfort that comes when the mind has had the courage to look realistically upon the world." We must, Ransom insists, have "ghosts in our employment who are to embody for us the aggregate force and tendency of the world as it bears upon our destiny" (314). In other words, if the God man creates is to be concrete, he must embody the harshness of the world as it actually is, and the Holy Ghost, as originally conceived, does precisely that. Ransom finds support for his position on the nature of existence in lines from a poem by A. E. Housman, the only poem quoted in the entire book:

> Therefore, since the world has still
> Much good, but much less good than ill,
> And while the sun and moon endure,
> Luck's a chance, but trouble's sure,
> I'd face it as a wise man should,
> And train for ill, but not for good.
>
> (315)

Ransom's fictional God, then, is as terrible as the universe Ransom inhabits.

In the epilogue that follows this vigorous and very lengthy apologia, however, Ransom presents a conclusion that "will seem a little bit ignominious as a climax to the study." He realizes sadly that the "Gods" are everywhere in trouble from the philosophers, scientists, and "naturalistic rabble" who want to usurp their place (319). Admitting that his characterization here is somewhat over-dramatized, he repeats that he is even more worried by the easy fraternizing that is taking place on some levels between science and religion, leading to a compromise with secularism and naturalism. But then, in a passage that stands isolated in the text and that cries out for a substantial effort to relate it to what has gone before, he is compelled to confess his own religious misgivings:

> We have moved far from the habits of those days and those climates to which the Scriptures were congenial. Culturally their language and their images seem strange to us now. . . . There is a real effort required now to enter into them sympathetically even when we consider that metaphysically they are sound. Perhaps we would greatly relish, and indeed it is probable that we are continually on the lookout to see if we will not discover somewhere, a brand new myth, not shopworn, not yet ridiculed, and not unrepresentative of what little taste we may have yet for the enjoyment of myths. But that is an event upon which it is impossible to make any calculations.   (324)

Obviously Ransom does not consider that he has succeeded in creating such a myth, and indeed it is precisely this kind of honest declaration that gives one insight into the extent to which he too shared in a thoroughly modern sensibility. His modest "solution" to the problem, until a satisfactory new myth is created, is that the faithful should simply return to their traditional churches and turn them from their false gods "whenever, and however, and so far as this proves practicable" (325).

It is difficult to judge to what extent Ransom was aware of the novelty of his position in *God Without Thunder* and whether he perceived it to be, as it certainly was, totally unorthodox, not only in the manner of the defense it offered—which Ransom never denied—but also in the understanding it revealed of that to which it claimed to be committed. From the evidence of the text, Ransom does not appear to have any kind of belief in God whatever; he even interchanges *god, God,* and *gods* on numerous occasions without misgiving or apology in the midst of his general argument for monotheism. It may be tempting, perhaps, to see a parallel with Paul de Man's claim that the assertions in Rousseau's *Profession de foi* "compel us to choose while destroying the foundations of any choice," but the problem is brought to no such crisis, and it seems more likely that Ransom genuinely thought that he had offered an explanation of the true basis of religion rather than significantly altered its intent.[3] Thus, in a letter to Robert Penn Warren in which he is commenting on a slightly earlier draft of the book, Ransom remarks, "I don't entirely believe in Romanism as Tate and other friends do"—a very puzzling statement unless one assumes that Ransom truly failed to appreciate the extent of his unorthodoxy (*SL*, 191). He would have to wait for the reviews of *God Without Thunder* before he would become aware of his miscalculation, and there is even a sense in which he never satisfactorily understood the real requirements of an orthodox belief.

Nevertheless, the writing of *God Without Thunder* had indeed provided Ransom with the opportunity to contemplate his previously unformulated ideas about religion. In doing so, it had also made him aware of their shortcomings—or perhaps of the extent to which he did not quite believe them in the manner in which they had been presented. Still, one can reasonably claim that already this book offers a definition of the kind of secular faith that Ransom was seeking and that, overtly, it had set out to condemn (witness

3. Paul de Man, *Allegories of Reading: Figural Language in Rousseau, Nietzsche, Rilke, and Proust* (New Haven, 1979), 245.

its many negative references to secular undertakings). Its basic message is that the aesthetic and ritualistic aspects of religion, when used properly, and preferably practiced in an agrarian setting, heighten man's awareness of the uncertainty and grimness of his destiny and by so doing make him more appreciative of that which is immediately available to him in the concreteness of nature. Indeed, Ransom's conclusion from the unresolvability of mathematical surds is that there is an "absoluteness somewhere" but that that somewhere is not in another world but rather in the concrete objects of our earthly experience: "It is quite true that absoluteness does not inhere in the objects regarded under the same kind, or by the same science: they become simply the quantities of a quality. But among the kinds, the qualities, the separate sciences, there is a variety which will not disappear. This variety focuses specifically in the concrete object, and inevitably causes it to exceed the simplicity with which the object is invested under any single system. *It confers upon the object the only absoluteness with which we are acquainted. The only absolute is the concrete object*" (285, my emphasis). The term *God*, then, is important only because with its rich historical associations it serves to express the glory and inexhaustibility of material objects.

For a while after *God Without Thunder* was published, however, Ransom actually attempted to practice the letter of what he preached by taking up a modified form of agrarian life just outside Nashville and by attending once again the Methodist services that he had long since abandoned. He was even persuaded to teach a Sunday-school class. His biographer, Thomas Daniel Young, describes the sequel:

> The students were impressed by his knowledge of the Scriptures and thoroughly approved of his attempts to focus the discussions always on specific passages from the Bible. A rather unpleasant situation arose, however, when several members of the class observed that Ransom did not join in the recitation of the Apostles' Creed. When he was pressed for an explanation, he admitted that he did not accept the trinitarian concept of the deity embodied in the creed; consequently he chose not to recite any of it. Some members of the class were disturbed by this revelation, and when he conveniently could, Ransom withdrew from teaching and soon stopped attending any of the other services at the church.

Ransom's rejection of the trinitarian doctrine was perfectly in keeping with the views expressed in *God Without Thunder*, wherein Christ is denied divinity. But it seems likely also that Ransom was coming to realize even more acutely some of the difficulties inherent in sustaining a religious faith on the grounds he had proposed. Besides, his refusal to recite a formula in which he himself did not believe—and one that he had specifically recommended in his book—indicates that he was still concerned with the truth or untruth of religious propositions and not simply with their pragmatic usefulness. So, as his biographer concludes: "Immediately thereafter he reverted to the pattern he had established after his return from Oxford nearly twenty years before. As long as his father was an active minister, he sometimes went to hear him preach. As a general rule, however, Sunday mornings were spent at home or on the golf course. Never again was he a member of the congregation of any church."[4]

Whatever its internal contradictions, and irrespective of whether or not it was more aesthetic than truly religious, the program set forth in *God Without Thunder* could best be carried out in an agrarian setting free from the "anodynes" of urban culture. Ransom's ideas, therefore, had practical social implications at a critical moment in American history when the industrial and financial complexes were in serious disarray. And Ransom devoted a good deal of his time during the early 1930s to promoting the agrarian way of life: he wrote several essays on the subject for national journals, engaged in public debates on its behalf, spent a year in England studying economics, and even on one occasion seriously considered founding a newspaper to advance the cause. Perhaps he most clearly indicated the connection between the aesthetic-religious sensibility and the agrarian way of life in his introduction to the famous collection of essays by Twelve Southerners entitled *I'll Take My Stand: The South and the Agrarian Tradition*, in which he states that while "religion is our submission to the general intention of a nature that is fairly inscrutable," nature industrialized "is no longer nature but a highly simplified picture of nature. We receive the illusion of having power over nature, and lose the sense of nature as something mysterious and contingent. The God of nature under these conditions is merely an amiable expression, a superfluity, and the philosophical understanding ordinarily carried in the religious experience is not there for us to have."[5] Agrarian conditions,

4. Young, *Gentleman in a Dustcoat*, 271–72.
5. Twelve Southerners, *I'll Take My Stand: The South and the Agrarian Tradition* (New York, 1930; rpr. Baton Rouge, 1977), xlii.

in contrast, serve to remind man of his true place in the universe and so are to be maintained and developed. But as the decade progressed and as Ransom conscientiously attempted to seek out practical solutions for the nation's economic ills, both his experiences and his studies led him—ever the true empiricist—to doubt that his agrarian project was feasible, or even desirable, in modern society, and so he gradually abandoned it to defend the aesthetic sensibility on more narrow, but also more philosophical, grounds.

By the mid-1930s, then, Ransom had finally come to terms with some of the specifically religious issues that perplexed him, and the agrarian movement was no longer of immediate concern to him. He was therefore at last free to pursue those aesthetic interests that he had temporarily put aside; he could, so to speak, descend from the thunder (which, as several contemporary reviews pointed out, was without God) to "the world's body," a phrase that he used for the title of his next book. More accurately, having treated the religious dimension of the aesthetic experience, he could turn to its parallel expressions in so-called secular poetry and examine to what extent they too either succeeded or failed. Certain poems, for example, might—like religion—be too Platonic, too interested in ideas, or, on the other hand, too concrete, too given over to images without sufficient attention to intellectual commentary. In elaborating, therefore, an ontology of the poetic experience, Ransom would find himself favoring the metaphysical poets of the seventeenth century over the moderns, who were too concerned with images, and most of all over the Victorians, who were too preoccupied with ideas—the most notorious example of the Victorian extreme, for Ransom, being the lines "God's in his heaven— / All's right with the world!" of Robert Browning's "Pippa Passes" (WB, 121). Metaphysical poetry, in contrast, "leaves us looking, marvelling, and revelling in the thick *dinglich* substance" of the world's "body" (WB, 142).[6] Moreover, this aesthetic appreciation could be heightened even further by the development of the kind of criticism that emphasized the closest reading possible of literary texts.

At the same time that Ransom's interests were moving more toward aesthetics, a resurgence of his old antagonistic attitude

6. René Wellek offers some interesting—if inconclusive—speculations, based in part on his correspondence with Ransom in 1971, about the philosophical origin of the word *dinglichkeit* in Ransom's writings (*American Criticism, 1900–1950*, 159–61).

toward religion appeared (though this had also been present in *God Without Thunder*). There is a note of censure, for instance, in the latter part of Ransom's insistence that "religion is an institution existing for the sake of its ritual, rather than, as I had heard, for the sake of its doctrines, to which there attaches no cogency of magic, and for that matter a very precarious cogency of logic." And again, Ransom now seems less confident about the rationality of belief than formerly:

> The issues upon which the doctrines pronounce are really insoluble for human logic, and the higher religionists are aware of it. The only solution that is possible . . . is the aesthetic one. When these issues [such as death] press upon us, there is little that one man, with whatever benefit of doctrines, can do toward the understanding of the event which another man cannot do; and he had better not try too hard to understand the precise event, but enlarge its terms, and assimilate it into the form of an ornate public ritual through which the whole mind can discharge itself. This is a subtle technique . . . in insisting upon it as the one thing I do not mean to subtract dignity from the world's great religions—which I revere.   (*WB*, 43)

The "higher religionists," temporarily condemned in *God Without Thunder* as secularists and compromisers, have been restored to grace, though one suspects that Ransom always reluctantly sympathized with their dilemma. Furthermore, mention of "the world's great religions" alerts one to Ransom's shift from allegiance to a single, fundamental belief, even if that belief is self-created: there is no longer one religion, but rather there are religions, and Ransom's concept is very close to Jungian eclecticism. Most noticeably of all, the religious / aesthetic sequence has been reversed to become the aesthetic / religious and thus to give priority to that which had been Ransom's chief concern all along.

Ransom realized, however, that there were serious problems ahead even for the survival of the aesthetic sensibility in its non-religious form. Referring to one of his favorite texts, Matthew Arnold's assertion that the future of poetry (as opposed to religion) is immense, Ransom comments that he does not mean "to seem too convinced about the immensity" (*WB*, 254). By 1939, he was prepared to admit that "the arts begin to stand today in the position which religion, an elder sister, was made to occupy during the last century: their disrepute in the intellectual circles increases almost at the rate at which philosophers find the time to attend to them" (*SE*, 107). Before arriving at a legitimate secular faith, therefore, he would have to come to terms with the objections of those he had referred to rather injudiciously in 1930 as the "naturalistic rabble"; and in the attempt to do so, he would find his own faith unexpectedly transformed as he experienced a major "shift of ideas."[7]

7. John Crowe Ransom, "The Poems of T. S. Eliot: A Perspective," *New Republic*, CXXVII (December 8, 1952), 16–17.

6

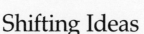

Shifting Ideas

"I do believe him to be an honest workman in a land teeming with blithering fake," Ezra Pound wrote Ford Madox Ford in 1937 when the latter requested a signature of support for Ransom, who was considering a move from Vanderbilt to Kenyon College in Ohio "to write poetry and teach philosophy."[1] Although Ford, then a guest of Allen Tate's in Tennessee, was unfair in his claim that "Ransom's departure has been forced by a very base University intrigue," the Kenyon offer came at a juncture when Ransom was increasingly anxious to turn his attention from an excessive involvement in the agrarian movement to those literary and philosophical pursuits that he had always found more congenial and that had begun to occupy him to a greater extent of late.[2] Since he now realized that the culture at large could not be changed in order to facilitate the aesthetic experiences of its members, henceforth he would see himself as belonging to "one of those minority cultural groups which have their rights in a free society as surely as individuals do." Appropriately enough in this light, when Ransom finally left Vanderbilt to take up his new appointment, he was followed by three

1. Brita Lindberg-Seyersted (ed.), *Pound / Ford: The Story of a Literary Friendship* (New York, 1982), 145–47; Young, *Gentleman in a Dustcoat*, 272. Pound's private commentary, however, was less flattering. On the other hand, when Ford had asked Ransom several years earlier to review Pound's poetry, Ransom wrote Tate that he was not "a Pound man" and that he agreed with Wyndham Lewis that "Pound is an ultra-conservative and classicist who has advertised all his life as a Revolutionist" (*SL*, 210).

2. Lindberg-Seyersted (ed.), *Pound / Ford*, 144. While it is true that Ransom was gradually moving away from "repetitive patriotism" at the time, Daniel Joseph Singal is misleading when he comments, "To minimize the pain—and to shed his southern and agrarian connections forever—Ransom moved in late 1937 from Vanderbilt to Kenyon College in Ohio" (*The War Within*, 219). Young's biography makes it clear that Ransom's move was characterized by confusion and misgiving.

of his most distinguished pupils: Randall Jarrell, Robert Lowell, and Peter Taylor. His unplanned departure from the South was to mark the beginning of a new phase in his intellectual life, one in which he would revise several of his earlier opinions as he tried to come to terms with the complex realities of the modern world. He was ready, as he wrote later, to question "the evidences which had led to my own personal set against the age."[3]

Ransom's intellectual development was due in part to the wider experience that became his as founder and editor of the *Kenyon Review* in 1938. This highly successful journal of arts and letters attracted an impressive range of contributors, many of them with views that were quite alien to those of Ransom himself. It is clear from his letters and other writings during his period as editor, 1939–1959, that his thinking was deeply stimulated by what came to him in the form of both requested and unrequested manuscripts from some of the best-known intellectuals of the day: Lionel Trilling, Theodor Adorno, Philip Rahv, William Barrett, Eric Bentley, Bertrand Russell, W. H. Auden, Henry D. Aiken, Jacques Maritain, Walter Kaufmann, R. P. Blackmur, Yvor Winters, Irving Howe, Conor Cruise O'Brien, Bertolt Brecht, Allen Tate, Paul Goodman, Charles Morris, Ernest Nagel, Robert Penn Warren, and others. Ransom was constantly on the lookout for new developments and rising reputations. And not surprisingly, he chose as his assistant editor a philosopher of rationalist and pragmatic persuasion, Philip Blair Rice.

The shift in Ransom's thinking that soon came about was by no means unprepared for. Although his formal rejection of agrarianism would not come until 1945, it is evident from his letters that his disenchantment with that movement had begun long before he left for Kenyon College.[4] Likewise, his change of position on the philosophy of naturalism was gradual and had been intimated in several of the essays in *The World's Body*. "Art and Mr. Santayana," for instance, which was first published in 1937, contains many of the same ideas found in the apparently more radical "The Inorganic Muses," which appeared in 1943. Again, Ransom was a keen Freudian even in the 1920s and had written enthusiastically about the

3. John Crowe Ransom, "The Communities of Letters," in *Poems and Essays* (New York, 1955), 116, and "The Poems of T. S. Eliot: A Perspective," 16.

4. See, for example, his letter to Tate of September 17, 1936, in whch he complains that "*patriotism* is eating at *lyricism*" (*SL*, 217).

psychoanalyst's work and defended him against the censures of Robert Graves. And, of course, his interest in the pragmatists was long standing.[5] Perhaps, then, the nuance of the change in his way of thinking is best conveyed in a statement from "The Inorganic Muses" in which Ransom stresses the impossibility of giving a transcendental explanation for organic activity: "We inherited from Plato, whose teachings were embodied in our theology, the notion of a separable, immortal, and inorganic soul. We inherited from Aristotle, through a tradition more metaphysical than theological, the notion of an intellect which works when the organism is not working, and independently of the organism and which therefore is also inorganic. But I believe that in effect, if not explicitly, we have let those heritages lapse, and do not need them. They may have done noble service in defending our humanistic progress, but they have served their purpose."[6] What this observation suggests is that while Ransom's fundamental ideas remained constant to a large extent, their theoretical elaborations altered considerably. He was in fact pursuing the logical consequences of the position for which he had argued in *God Without Thunder* —that not only God, but also such metaphysical entities as souls and spirits are to be understood purely as necessary fictions. The question that frequently comes to mind as one proceeds through his essays of the forties, fifties, and sixties is whether or not he has conceded too much to those he formerly believed to be the enemy. Has he, as Tate feared, stumbled into a quagmire from which it would be impossible to salvage any nonutilitarian values whatever?

In one of his first essays in the *Kenyon Review*, "The Arts and the Philosophers," Ransom restates the case that natural science has convicted religion of uttering falsehood, but then claims that "art is much more protean and elusive than any established religion can be; they [the natural scientists] will find it harder to obtain conviction, and impossible to keep the prisoner long confined" (*SE*, 111). Nevertheless, he feels it necessary to contribute to the philosophical justification of poetry in a world that is inclined toward naturalism. In his somewhat awkward formulation, poetry aims

5. See, for example, his reviews of Freud's *Beyond the Pleasure Principle* and *Group Psychology* in *Saturday Review of Literature*, I (October 4, 1924), 161–62.

6. John Crowe Ransom, "The Inorganic Muses," *Kenyon Review*, V (Spring, 1943), 284, hereinafter cited parenthetically by page number in the text.

at providing "the kind of knowledge by which we must know what we have arranged that we shall not know otherwise"; it helps man "to realize the world, to see it better" (WB, x). There is, in Ransom's view, nothing else to see. Thus the challenges of those who would attack poetry by claiming either that man can "see" a lot more—the religionists—or that he can "see" a lot less—the positivists (for whom poetry is nonsense)—need to be answered. One can therefore think of Ransom throughout the 1940s as fighting off, on the one hand, the dogmatic religionists and, on the other, the extreme positivists, as he tries to maintain some middle ground for the aesthetic apprehension, which is the only "faith" to which he can commit himself. Positivism, pragmatism, and naturalism are, according to Ransom in "The Inorganic Muses," philosophies that "overlap each other confusingly, and in fact they are developments within a single impulse" that is basically antimetaphysical, opposed to the "reifying of adjectives" and the unnecessary "multiplying of the entities" (280). The surprise is that the positivists are partly successful in winning Ransom to their side.

Although Ransom had, of course, been sympathetically following the progress of logicians and generally empiricist thinkers such as Dewey and Russell for years, the immediate occasion for his current interest in the positivists—or, more accurately, with the naturalist and pragmatist wings of the movement—was the publication of a number of pamphlets from the *International Encyclopedia of Unified Science*, which was based at the University of Chicago under the general editorship of Otto Neurath, Rudolf Carnap, and Charles Morris. The encyclopedia, which, as its title implies, aimed at finding a common ground among the various sciences, was the work of former members of the Vienna Circle, the source of the logical-positivist movement in philosophy. Several of the founders of this radically antimetaphysical group, which at various times included Neurath, Carnap, Russell, Wittgenstein, A. J. Ayer, and Morris (not all of whom were equally associated with it), had been forced to migrate to the United States in the mid-thirties. The encyclopedia therefore offered the "official" version of positivistic philosophy, and so Ransom eagerly solicited some of the pamphlets in order to get a debate under way in the first issues of the *Kenyon Review* (SL, 256). But whereas he began as a potential antagonist, he ended as a cautious partisan, at least when dealing with his former allies who tended to be totally opposed to the new movement.

A quotation from Dewey's contribution to the first volume of the encyclopedia indicates the kind of sentiment with which Ransom was to become increasingly sympathetic during this period. Although there were several aspects of the project with which Dewey himself was not in agreement, he did at least share its antimetaphysical bias:

The word "metaphysics" has many meanings, all of which are generally supposed to be so highly technical as to be of no interest to the man in the street. But in the sense that "metaphysical" means that which is outside of experience, over and beyond it, all human beings are metaphysical when they occupy themselves with problems which do not rise out of experience and for which solutions are sought outside experience. Men are metaphysical not only in technical philosophy but in many of their beliefs and habits of thought in religion, morals, and politics. The waste of energy that results is serious enough. But this is slight compared with that which is wrought by artificial problems and solutions in preventing, deflecting, and distorting the development of the scientific attitude which is the proper career of intelligence.[7]

It is easy to see that this appeal to experience was attractive to a thinker like Ransom. Moreover, in spite of their declared hostility to any mode of language that claimed a nonempirical reference, what the positivists appeared to offer was a potentially scientific foundation for art and religion, or at least one that Ransom thought he could adapt to such purposes. In 1939, he even went so far as to propose to Tate that they themselves found the *Encyclopedia of Unified Art and Religion* on the model of the positivist encyclopedia (*SL*, 256). Although the project never got under way, nearly all of Ransom's essays over the next ten years were to be permeated either explicitly or implicitly with some reference to a philosophy of generally positivistic inclination.

In his next book, then, entitled *The New Criticism*, Ransom sets

7. John Dewey, "Unity of Science as a Social Problem," in Otto Neurath, Rudolf Carnap, and Charles Morris (eds.), *Foundations of the Unity of Science* (Chicago, 1971), 32. The original pamphlets began appearing in 1938. In "The New Encyclopedists," *Kenyon Review*, (Spring, 1939), 168, Eliseo Vivas describes the movement as "not the youthful positivism of yesterday, myopic, narrow, and often petulant, but a mature positivism which has been happily wedded, through Morris' work on meaning, to the rich tradition of pragmatism and which will therefore share pragmatism's fundamental interest in human values." Nevertheless, "while it calls attention to the fact that we need not turn into utter nonsense statements made in the language of fable, myth, or poetry, it does give the consistent empiricist good grounds for denying semantic meaning to terms which claim to refer to transempirical objects which cannot be reduced to objects of experience" (165).

out to defend the claim that poetry is a form of knowledge against
the rival views of those critics who would lay emphasis on its other
aspects: I. A. Richards, concerned with its psychological effects;
Eliot, preoccupied with certain historical and religious problems
related to it; and Yvor Winters, "a victim of the moralistic illusion"
(NC, xi). In the book's concluding essay, "Wanted: An Ontological
Critic," Ransom presents his own point of view, and his gradual
shift in a positivistic direction is particularly noticeable. There he
acknowledges that since poetry is "a revolutionary departure from
the convention of logical discourse," one that aims at recovering
"the denser and more refractory original world which we know
loosely through our perceptions and memories," and since it treats
"an order of existence" that cannot be dealt with in scientific discourse, it requires "a bold and proportionate designation" (NC,
280–81). Ransom chooses Morris, author of Foundations of the Theory of Signs (part of Volume I of Neurath's International Encyclopedia
of Unified Science), for guidance in his task. Morris is especially
promising because he indeed claims that there are "three irreduc-
ible forms of discourse: science, art, and technology" (NC, 238).
The distinction peculiar to art is that its signs are iconic in that they
in some way resemble the objects to which they refer. But, according to Ransom, Morris fails to see the implication of his own assertion, namely, that the object referred to by an iconic sign is imag-
inable but not definable—hence the ontological separateness of
artistic discourse. Nevertheless, Morris' exposition is "another evidence of what I have hoped for: the capacity of radical modernist
philosophy to apprehend and testify to kinds of truth that do not
necessarily suit its own preoccupations" (NC, 286).

Both Ransom and Tate were studying Morris in the early 1940s
and corresponding regularly about their findings. Tate's resultant
essay, "Literature as Knowledge," is in marked contrast to Ransom's
in that he is much less sympathetic with Morris' theories, finally
accusing him of being a behaviorist who denies cognition. Tate objects to what he conceives of as a psychological tradition that runs
rather diffusely from Coleridge through Arnold, Dewey, Richards,
and Morris and that betrays a "general attitude towards experience" that is positivistic.[8] Not only did Ransom feel more favorably

8. Allen Tate, "Literature as Knowledge," Southern Review, VI (Spring, 1941),
629–57.

disposed toward this sequence of critics—though by no means without qualification—but he became quite preoccupied with the details of the argument. When "Wanted: An Ontological Critic" appeared a short time after Tate's essay, it seemed to some that Ransom had been much too sympathetic toward the positivists. On April 14, 1941, therefore, he wrote a long letter to Tate in which he defended Morris, concluding: "I incline to judge that 'his heart is in the right place.' In other words, he is better than Carnap, and a lot of others of his own crowd. . . . My own feeling about them is one of watchful waiting, not entirely unfriendly. They are pretty much 'fed up' on the philosophical classics, but who is not? They represent starting at the bottom, and pedagogically I rather think that is the right thing now" (*SL*, 279–80).

A month later Ransom felt compelled to write again to Tate on the same subject:

> I don't think the Positivists will regard me as a convert, unless they are grateful for very small favors, which I think they are not. They have nothing as yet to show by way of poetic analysis. But they may turn out to have something when they get round to it. . . . I am forced to regard poetic theory as science, though a new science, because about a new or "different" kind of discourse. That's why I don't want any taboos, restrictions, philosophical censorship, against the analytic work. If that is Positivism, I guess I'm a member of the tribe. But so far as the absurd emphasis on scientific discourse as the only discourse goes, I'm far from being one.   (*SL*, 282)

Ransom is grateful to the positivists for their development of semantical theory, something that critics such as Richards, William Empson, and Kenneth Burke have been able to use for poetic appreciation. Yet, though he claims that this is all he expects from the positivists, it is clear that he has in some deeper way subscribed to that "general attitude towards experience" decried by Tate.

Nowhere at the time was this change more apparent than in Section VI of "T. S. Eliot: The Historical Critic," the second essay in *The New Criticism*. The threat from Eliot, as opposed to the positivists, is that he has become excessively attached to the spurious authority of religious dogmas. He does not seem to accept the notion expressed in *God Without Thunder* that religious propositions are simply necessary myths. Ransom therefore needs to refute this writer's influential views if he is to establish the validity of his own poetic theory, and, in addition, his commitment to a generic variety of humanism. Thus he begins his essay by lamenting the fact that Eliot both as poet and as critic has been moving farther and farther away from his early aesthetic independence, in which even the "irreligious poet" and the "godless Elizabethans" commanded his sympathies (NC, 138). Section VI then offers a brilliantly subtle, yet surprisingly passionate criticism of Eliot's attitudes.

Ransom's attack consists basically of two parts, which are, however, closely related. In the first, he tries to show that Eliot's objections to contemporary humanists such as Irving Babbitt (Eliot's old teacher at Harvard) and Norman Foerster do not have much merit in the kind of intellectual climate that exists at present. In the second, Ransom argues that poetic statements are just as valid as those proper to religion.

Eliot had criticized the humanism of Babbitt's *Democracy and Leadership*, which appeared in 1924, from the point of view of the Western religious tradition: "Humanism has been sporadic, but Christianity continuous." Ransom comments:

> This is not a position without dignity. . . . But it did not prove effective with Mr. Babbitt, in the sequel; nor is its effectiveness very considerable with many able minds who are not now so religiously inclined by heredity and training as they might be, but tainted with naturalistic aversions and positivistic hopes; and calling for everybody to put his cards upon the table so that everything may be settled on its merits. In the pack with which they are playing is no card named the religious tradition. With this hard breed of thinkers, laying out a new world, the argument from tradition does not rate as a philosophical argument.   (196–97)

This passage has a little of the flavor of that final section of *God Without Thunder* in which Ransom briefly and rather poignantly admits his own religious misgivings and his inability to surrender his modern critical sensibility.

Ransom is even more provoked by Eliot's attack on Foerster. Foerster had claimed that "the value of supernatural intuition must be tested by the intellect." Eliot contended that this had always been the tradition of the Church and that Foerster's attacks were "a composition of ignorance, prejudice, confused thinking and bad writing." Ransom chides him slyly: "We understand the limitations of any essay, yet Eliot might have had more to say to Mr. Foerster than this; he might have assumed that Mr. Foerster had himself done some thinking, and even informed himself about the test made by the Church before he and his group of philosophers were born, but was not satisfied with it" (198–99). To Eliot's argument that the intellectual acceptance of religious dogma is much easier than Foerster supposes and that understanding comes with the actual practice of belief, Ransom cautions:

> Once more, I think it a good argument if it will work. But I suggest that the argument from tradition will not work now as it used to; that we are dealing with a revolutionary party which happens to comprise a large proportion of the intellectuals of our age; and that a more explicit and philosophical argument is necessary if we propose to have any effect. . . . I confess incidentally, and since I do not mean to assume that I have any advantages over Mr. Eliot, that the difficulties faced by the religious establishments are difficulties which I feel equally in the sense that I deplore them, and that I cannot solve them. But I am not quite so mistrustful of the naturalists and positivists as he is.   (200)

Ransom does not deal with the rather obvious point that whereas Eliot was attempting to defend a religion believed to have eternal validity whether or not a particular generation of mankind accepted it, he himself was involved in the altogether different task of arguing for religion as a form of knowledge that answered man's perennial psychic needs.

Ransom admits over and over again that he is sympathetic with the sentiments of Eliot and Tate in regard to religion. He quotes a recent attack by Tate on the supposed inadequacies of historicism, psychologism, and scientism. But then he is compelled to indicate his own misgivings about such an approach in a passage that marks the first of his explicit revisions:

> I have said probably nearly as much, and more than once; but increasingly now I feel that such a policy is too luxurious for my blood. The forces that have captured the world are trying to found a new civilization, and I imagine about that, first, that it is going to be much harder than they suppose to get everything into it, and, second, that when they have got a new civilization it may turn out to be oddly like the old one. . . . But I am often impressed by their honesty, and also by the sense that they are making some headway.   (201)

Ransom offers Dewey (whose influence Tate had referred to as "a powerful aid to the coming of the slave society") as an example of such an honest thinker who incorporates into his philosophy everything in art, morals, and religion that Eliot would wish for. Although Dewey may not care much for tradition, Ransom cannot any longer consider such an attitude a "monstrous villainy" even if a "very stiff" Eliot would wish to do so (202).

Eliot's opposition to a secular humanism, of course, was based ultimately on his belief that there had been a divine revelation in history. Thus in "Arnold and Pater," he attacked Arnold for "subtracting from religion its intellectual affirmations" and reducing them to mere poetry. But Ransom inclines rather to identify with Arnold in the judgment that the German higher criticism has made it quite impossible to believe in biblical events in the way in which former generations did (202–203). What he finds irritating in Eliot is that the latter would sacrifice the "facts" of poetic discourse while attempting to preserve them for religion. Ransom's view is that the "facts" of religion and poetry are both speculative fictions with equal validity, though religious dogma "differs radically from the merely poetic myth" insofar as it is required to support the popular morality. Religious dogma, however, cannot claim to be any more "supernatural" than a scientific hypothesis and, in that it does make such claims, it is necessarily unacceptable:

> But there is a difference between saying "hypothesis" and saying "revelation." Probably the better thing we have gained from our progress in science has not been some substantive or material benefit, but a methodological one. We know how we are thinking when we think; we can think critically, self-consciously, and with the intent not to deceive ourselves. Science, at its not too rare best, can do its thinking with complete awareness of when it resorts to hypothesis. And another name for hypothesis is speculation. But religion is reluctant to concede that its "revealed truth" is speculation. . . . Religionists, we may imagine, have been keenly aware of (1) the practical importance of their speculations for the whole population, and (2) the impossibility of arguing them with the brilliant precision which so much impresses the public in favor of the natural sciences. These two considerations might well have persuaded religionists to propose the artificial sanction of "revelation." The speculations become sacrosanct. But the history of thought would indicate that this is a status which cannot perpetuate itself.   (206–207)

As an account of the historical origins of the concept of revelation, Ransom's remarks are, of course, wildly inaccurate. That is hardly what he intended to offer, however. What he is pointing to is a serious problem that religion has in an intellectual climate tinged with naturalism—a problem that the higher critics of the nineteenth century set out to solve with their new hermeneutics. Ransom therefore extends his criticism to make a brief comment on the desperate position of the churches "perhaps proportionately to the degree of arrogance with which they cite their mandatory revelations, against a generation which is acutely conscious of methodological standards in its thinking." They will have to abandon their dogmas or be themselves abandoned, though he is hopeful—more than Eliot, he thinks—that "speculative generalizations" with "religious significance" can be salvaged. This, he says, is "a word of personal testimony" (207).

Ransom finally restates the case that his basic disagreement is with Eliot's assertion that in religion sincere belief is important, while in poetry only the reader's temporary assent to the poet's faith is required:

> [Eliot] believes in believing the religious dogmas, not the affirmations of poetry. I can see no necessity for waiving the intellectual standards on behalf of poets. If Dante's beliefs cannot be accepted by his reader, it is the worse for Dante with that reader, not a matter of indifference as Eliot has argued. If Shelley's argument is foolish, it makes his poetry foolish. In my mind Dante's beliefs are very bold speculations at which the accusing finger has pointed steadily for a long time now, but substantively are better grounded, and methodologically far more consistent, than Shelley's beliefs. That consideration would enter into my preference of Dante over Shelley.   (207–208)

As always, Ransom regards religious and poetic beliefs as being on an equal speculative footing already and in need of the same kind of defense and subject to the same kind of empirical constraints. Dante is preferred to Shelley, therefore, because Dante's sober view of the universe, though outdated in many respects, is judged to be truer to experience than that of the Promethean Romantic.

Ransom's claims in this essay are not all that new, but when placed in opposition to those of a strong religionist such as Eliot, they appear perhaps more radical than they seemed in his earlier writings. Certainly, however, "T. S. Eliot: The Historical Critic" marks a shift of emphasis from *God Without Thunder* in the direction of the naturalists and positivists, and toward a proclamation of Ransom's own aesthetic faith. *Positivist* and *naturalist* will appear in almost every subsequent essay, and Ransom's characteristic stance will be that of defender of these metascientists against the specious metaphysics of Eliot or Tate or Maritain. Although Ransom frequently agrees with these three writers in terms of the values they are seeking to uphold, he takes issue with the procedures they use to do so. It could be argued from their point of view, however, that he still does not seem to be aware of what a radical revision of

the concept of traditional religion would be required by his pro-
posals, or of the serious logical problems that would ultimately result from them.[9]

Sometime in late 1942 or early 1943, when Ransom received the
poems and accompanying philosophical essay that were the fruits
of Robert Lowell's recent conversion to Catholicism, he was working hard—as he informed Lowell—on his "Maritain-naturalism-
Eliot" paper (*SL*, 308). Ransom's essay, which appeared shortly
afterwards in the *Kenyon Review* under the title "The Inorganic
Muses," provides the most important account available of his own
philosophical position in the 1940s and of its differences from the
positions of Maritain and Eliot. Maritain, then enjoying a measure
of success in artistic and academic religious circles in the United
States and Canada for his appealing version of neo-Thomism (which
had profoundly influenced both Tate and Lowell), had recently
contributed an essay entitled "Poetry's Dark Night" to the *Kenyon
Review*, thus giving Ransom a suitable foil for the exposition of his
own point of view on the same topics. "The Inorganic Muses"
offers the first explicit declaration of Ransom's secular faith, *secular*
being the term he himself uses in this context.

Ransom's sympathy with the antimetaphysical arguments of the
positivists and naturalists is shown first of all in his criticisms of
Maritain's style of writing, even while he agrees with much of what
the French philosopher is saying about the problems of modern
poetry. Typical of Maritain's essay is the following:

> Poetry is ontology—indeed; and we may even say, in the great phrase of
> Boccaccio, poetry is theology. But only in the sense that it is born in the

9. The same kinds of problems arise also from Richard Rorty's somewhat similar concept of a "post-philosophical" culture, in which "no particular portion of culture [such as philosophy or theology] would be singled out as exemplifying (or sig-
nally failing to exemplify) the condition to which the rest aspired. There would be
no sense that, beyond the current intra-disciplinary criteria, which, for example,
good priests or good physicists obeyed, there were other, transdisciplinary, trans-
cultural, ahistorical criteria, which they also obeyed" (*Consequences of Pragmatism*
[Minneapolis, 1982], xxxviii). It would seem that in such a culture the priests at least
would have to make a rather dramatic shift in their interpretation of the origins of
their doctrines, one that would soon relieve them of their sacerdotal duties, though
it might well reinstall them as professional psychologists, sociologists, counselors,
professors, and so on—as, indeed, has happened widely in the present culture. It is
difficult to see how they could continue to carry on as *priests*, and this is the question that both Ransom and Rorty fail to address.

soul at the mysterious sources of being and reveals them, after a fashion, by its proper creative motion. If the unconscious from which it proceeds is not, except secondarily, the Freudian unconscious of instincts and images, it is nevertheless a more vital and profound unconscious, the unconscious of the spirit *at its source*—hidden from the inquisitive intelligence in that density of the soul where all spiritual faculties have their common origin.[10]

Ransom begins his commentary: "I should not undertake to write the equivalent of his [Maritain's] essay, for among other limitations I am not a master of the kind of language he uses. It has a literary quality which I admire and of which at the same time I confess I am afraid; a quality often found in the language of 'metaphysical' philosophers. An aggressive and dedicated metaphysics seems to me almost something magnificently chimerical . . . and deserving of many of the well-known strictures of the Naturalists. M. Maritain's variety of metaphysics does not alter this impression" (278–79).

The trouble with Maritain's dense metaphysical language is that "it creates substances for the metaphysical philosophy, or gods and 'personifications' for religion and mythos," and that such an approach is no longer defensible—at least in that precise form—in an age of prose (281). Ransom is acutely aware of his own intellectual development in this matter, a development that has been partly brought about through his study of Dewey, who is "making the closest effort to honor the artist and determine what proper human thing he can be doing with nature":

> It has grown more and more upon me, at the expense of the strong prejudices which my old-line education drilled into me, to conceive human activities naturalistically. For I believe we actually and always do question the "motives" of strange activities, and are not satisfied till we can identify them within those common motor activities which might be described as staple, biotic, vital, animal, organic, constitutional, or by other such adjectives. And suppose the question arises: Is man not capable of "transcending" his animal constitution? That would make him capable of original special motivations not connected with his vital processes. But how then could he ever have a rule for distinguishing between what belonged to his biotic self and what belonged to his bloodless and transcendental ego? And would not the latter, if seriously competing with the former, be apt to destroy it? Prepossessed as we now are by principles derived from our long biological studies, I should say that we are not so enterprising as seriously to assert that such a capability is feasible or even possible for man.   (284)

10. Jacques Maritain, "Poetry's Dark Night," *Kenyon Review*, V (Autumn, 1943), 158.

There is no longer a need for the metaphysical structures of Plato and Aristotle to protect a humanistic civilization such as presently exists. As if to underline his revised attitude, Ransom confesses:

> If it used to seem to me that anthropologists were despicable cynics peering and slandering in order to report animal origins behind the most exalted human activities, that was in my Platonic and metaphysical days; and now I think perhaps the sternest judgments of the race pronounce upon our precious activities by this criterion, and by no other. It is as though the judgment flowed from the racial instinct and would not betray its origins. I hope it may be a sign of maturity in a literary critic, and not merely a tactical shift, to be disposed to acknowledge specifically the humble origins, and the homely responsibilities, of his art.

Although Ransom has "long been ready to make this acknowledgment," he has been "deterred chiefly by my reading of some actual obtuse anthropologists—and Naturalists" (285).

The problem that remains, however, is how to account for poetry and religion in a naturalistic context. As universal activities, they simply exist and cannot be ignored, and therefore require some kind of explanation. Ransom thinks that the prose element in poetry can certainly be justified: "A poetic discourse embodies within itself, and intends not to lose or vitiate, a prose discourse. I think this is a law of poetry if there are laws of poetry, and takes precedence over any other law. No prose argument, no poem. I should subscribe to the modern philosophies to the extent of believing that we cannot accept a poetry . . . which does not record some contribution to the biotic organism" (286). The prose statement of a poem, insofar as it indicates a particular judgment about the world, can in principle be validated.

More problematic by far than the prose element—which Ransom calls "structure"—is that "excess" of imagistic language peculiar to poetry, its "texture." Such rhetorical colorings are "evasions of the logical line [of the poem] such as careless and unphilosophical readers do not ordinarily detect" (289). Ransom's response here is, first, that the "insubordinate detail" that makes for the richness of poetry does not fly in the face of the poem's prose argument and, second, that even in nature itself one finds similar excesses—a dog, for example, can be attached to its master beyond his usefulness as its "meal-ticket." Ransom elaborates on this point rather humorously, though he is quite serious about the basic intent of his illustration: "The dog is like a poet in doing more than expect and calculate his creature benefits from the object; for example, the smell of the master's tobacco must be 'vivid' to him yet without organic meaning. And the dog is a sort of religionist in the degree that the master's purposes and techniques remain inscrutable, and the dog's regard for them is speculative and humble" (291–92). Poetry, therefore, like religion, is an "organic-and-inorganic" activity insofar as it both relates and does not relate to the activity of the human organism. But Ransom cautions that neither poetry nor religion should interfere with man's primary organic activities: "The poem is not a poem except as it subscribes to a proper or organic 'operation.' It seems also that a religious affirmation, so much like a poetic one when the poet's terms are of cosmic dimension, does not start, and cannot sustain itself, except in the light of the current public scientific understanding. We indulge our aesthetic interests on the understanding that the organic interests will be respected, and have already been secured" (291).

Consequently, the modern French poets with whom Maritain was concerned, Baudelaire and Rimbaud, who "seem not to accept the humble organic-and-inorganic idea but to aspire towards a completely inorganic poetry" are wasting "much brilliant effort" in attempting the impossible (293). So is T. S. Eliot, for many of his poems do not appear to have a logical structure and therefore make no contribution to the human organism. Ransom's hope is that Eliot will renounce his preoccupation with obscure religious "symbols" and devote himself instead to "a much more secular poetry" (298). Ransom in fact sees signs of "a new secular freshness" in "Burnt Norton," though it still contains "many mystifications" (300). The essay makes clear, however, that it is really Ransom himself who has become secular in his attempt at reconciling his artistic and religious interests with the demands of contemporary philosophical naturalism.

Like *God Without Thunder*, "The Inorganic Muses" partly represents one of Ransom's regular efforts at contemplating his own current position before he makes his next move. The nuances of his attitude are expressed again in a letter to Tate in 1943. Confessing that he does not really care what the positivists, pragmatists, or naturalists think about his theories, he continues:

> I like the naturalistic approach to anthropology provided it's an open and honest one; I should want to found a non-Positivist activity firmly in the human constitution, otherwise it's just a vagary. (The Positivists

have the most elemental, most central, and best view of what all human conduct is biographically, or with respect to its purpose, technique, and morality.) . . . I could never be a Positivist, however, except as I was a scientist; the Positivists explicitly declare there is no kind of discourse except the scientific one. The Naturalists seem more open-minded. . . . I have no self-consciousness as to whether I sound like a Positivist or a Naturalist; let people read me to see if I am one. . . . I do not see any necessity to reject them automatically and go on record in some heroic manner. On nearly every page I write I am careful to write in my reservations with regard to common doctrine. But I would have to have a doctrine never heard of before, and new at all points, in order to make sweeping rejections of common doctrines.   (SL, 304)

The naturalists and positivists are simply those most adaptable to Ransom's purposes of working out what he later refers to as an aesthetic (as opposed to theological) faith. Thus again, for example, when Russell published a short essay, "Non-Materialistic Naturalism," in the Kenyon Review, Ransom agreed with his basic premises that the mind is nothing but a "certain series of events" that cease with the disintegration of the body at death, and that if there is a God, then his purposes are quite different from mankind's and can give no comfort; but he then went on to criticize the English philosopher from his own perspective:

> It would seem to be evident now that theologians cannot conceive their tropes any longer, if they have done so, as devices to evade nature, producing special eschatological benefits for example, or other practical advantages better than the formulations of honest science can furnish. They will not escape strictures like those which Mr. Russell makes against theology as the bogus science he contemns. Yet we are intellectually compelled in some way to embrace in our picture of nature just that chaos which invests and blunts the gallant universals. . . . If myth seems to say this, it is plainer to religionists and literary men than to Mr. Russell and many another philosopher.[11]

Indeed, even Russell's reference to "non-materialistic naturalism" must have seemed excessively tinged with philosophical idealism to a poet of Ransom's profoundly materialistic persuasion.[12]

11. Bertrand Russell, "Non-Materialistic Naturalism," Kenyon Review, IV (Autumn, 1942), 363–64; John Crowe Ransom, "Mr. Russell and Mr. Schorer," Kenyon Review, IV (Autumn, 1942), 406–407.

12. Ransom tended to be more naturalistic than the so-called naturalists themselves, contending that they were insufficiently interested in matter and, "when they begin to have ontological exercises," inclined rather toward Hegelian idealism, whereas a poet like Yeats, working with "objects and forms of discourse advertising extreme heterogeneity," offered an example of "naturalism proper" ("The Irish, the

In subsequent years this "perennial subject," as he referred to it, would continue to occupy Ransom. In "Art Worries the Naturalists," published in 1945, for example, he again declares that he "used to regard naturalism as a specially malignant heresy" but that now he thinks the dispute is partly verbal; at worst, naturalism is suffering from "immaturity." Defenders of the movement, such as George Santayana and Dewey, are "major figures, if there are any, which our country has contributed to the world's philosophy." [13] In a similar piece, also published in 1945, Ransom makes his famous revision of his agrarian philosophy of earlier years. The revision, made in the context of a reply to a pro-agrarian essay by a former student of his that had appeared in the *Kenyon Review,* indicates just how fully aware Ransom was of the practical demands of the life around him: "Without consenting to a division of labor, and hence modern society, we should have not only no effective science, invention, and scholarship, but nothing to speak of in art, e.g. *reviews* and contributions to *reviews,* fine poems and their exegesis" (*SE,* 189).

Ransom opens "Beating the Naturalists with the Stick of Drama" in the same year by informing his readers that S. L. Bethell, whose *Shakespeare and the Popular Dramatic Tradition* he is criticizing, "pursued literary and theological studies" at Cambridge. This, Ransom conjectures, may be the reason why Bethell's antinaturalism "is of the common or garden variety: super-naturalism." When Bethell wonders if, in *King Lear,* Shakespeare is putting nature forward in its less appealing aspect so as "to present a world without revelation, in order to determine how far human nature could penetrate its mysteries and achieve religious and moral order apart from the gift of supernatural grace," Ransom comments dryly, "This defiant last phrase is as beguiling, it is as truly Romantic and evasive, as it is venerable and official." Bethell might have done better "if he had

---

Gaelic, the Byzantine," *Southern Review,* VII [1941–1942], 546). In this essay also, Ransom attacks modern aesthetics as derived from Kant and Hegel because it parallels the rise of science and so presents ideas as ruling over brute matter: "It becomes the cult of the unifying form. Perhaps the greatest historical exception that has been taken was the diversion created by Nietzsche, who advanced his Dionysian principle; in effect it was the cult of nature as against the Apollonian cult of form which had monopolized the show hitherto" (540).

13. Ransom, "Art Worries the Naturalists," in *Beating the Bushes,* 93–94. Ransom is critical, however, of Dewey's attempts, in Hegelian fashion, to square "nature" entirely with "rational human action" (106).

said nothing about supernaturalism" and had attempted instead a "close psychological study of the concrete operation of this sensibility" for dramatic verse. "It might have consequences for all our aesthetic theories, and even cast a belated illumination upon the processes of our troubled religious consciousness."[14] In other words, psychological study, not an appeal to supernatural principles, is likely to enlighten man's current darkness.

Again, in "Poetry: II. The Final Cause," published in 1947, Ransom repeats his now familiar theme: "I am horrified by the horror which is still being professed toward these new philosophies by apologists of poetry, as of religion. But I think it too intransigent of us, and I am afraid it will be quaint, to deny all recent ways of thinking. I should say that logical positivism is a rather specialized philosophy, but that is not true of naturalism. In naturalistic speculation, a man is nothing less than a biological and psychological organism. I cannot see why he should be more; provided of course the whole man can be figured organically, including the poet in man" (SE, 226–27). In searching for an empirical basis for the poetic impulse, he turns this time to Freud and declares that it is a manifestation of the Id ("texture") in control of the Ego ("structure"). Ransom adds that Freud "carefully blue-printed the possible neural mechanisms which would support the conscious-unconscious compounds of behavior" (SE, 229). In spite of its now questionable accuracy, this reference confirms Ransom's own continuing commitment to empiricism at all levels—a commitment that would be evident again some twenty years later in his remarks on the experiential justification for Eliot's "still moments."

It is in keeping with this general attitude that in a review entitled "The New Criticism" in 1948, Ransom takes his friend Richard Blackmur to task for his denunciation of psychology, anthropology, and sociology as "dubious and precarious skills" that "undermine purpose, blight consciousness, and prevent decision":

> The consideration which I should want to urge upon Blackmur would be this: whether psychology, anthropology, and sociology, though they are not now and probably do not ever hope to be the precision instruments that are coveted popularly, are not the most effective means for studying the given distress. I do not suggest that the distress can be identified by a word, or even a phrase, but that we may come nearest to

14. Ransom, "Beating the Naturalists with the Stick of Drama," in *Beating the Bushes*, 125, 126, 127.

identifying it with their help. They are just newer than the distress it-self, and it is as if they had been called into being precisely in order to deal with that baffling object.[15]

According to Ransom, it is the synthesis of such skills that will ulti-mately help solve the present crisis.

Ransom's position, then, at the end of the 1940s seems to have consisted in a reconciliation with the naturalists, a desire to defend poetry in empirical terms, and an irritation with those religionists who rejected naturalism completely. Ransom believed that "prog-ress" was probably inevitable: "The movement from ritual to ro-mance, and from romance to naturalism seems to be according to the line of human progress, and perhaps on the whole the line can be traversed in only one direction. Doubtless this is just as bad as it is good. But it is a linguistic phenomenon; a matter of translating from an earlier language into a later. In the course of this transla-tion nothing that is valid need be given up for lost, for the value was always that of a symbol whose referent was something that 'took place' in the natural world" (SE, 234). Here Ransom is simply restating his nominalist philosophy: the world of experience re-mains the same while the terms by which it is interpreted change from age to age. It is, according to him, unfortunately the case that the present age is not a religious one.

15. John Crowe Ransom, "The New Criticism," *Kenyon Review*, X (Autumn, 1948), 684–85.

7

A Secular Faith

"By the way, there's such a St. Paul Society drive on our campus," Ransom informed Arthur Mizener in the spring of 1954, "that theology is destroying literary criticism in my present class, so that one pretty good man concludes a paper on Hardy about like this: 'In short, Thomas Hardy declined the gift which the Church offered to him; to wit, Eternal Life.' How is the grader to contrive a marginal note on that paper?" How indeed! Especially when one's own mind has become, as Ransom had written Tate two years earlier, "stubbornly secular."[1] For, just at the time when, to Ransom, there seemed to be a "religious revival among the intellectuals" (one indication of which was a renewed interest in the works of George Herbert), he himself had arrived at an overall conclusion to the problems that had been occupying him for so many years—a conclusion that was of course quite the opposite in its intention. Or at least he was ready to give a clearer, one might even say formulaic, statement of what he had been thinking for a long time. Now it was Wallace Stevens who was the great poet of the age, and he was such precisely because of his appeal to its secular character. The poems of this writer of "intellectual maturity," Ransom argues, "from the first volume onward may be construed as a set of Notes Toward the Definition of a Secular Culture and would therefore stand in some opposition to T. S. Eliot's Notes Toward the Definition of a Culture as Based on Religion."[2] Stevens, according

1. John Crowe Ransom to Arthur Mizener, May 26, 1954, in John Crowe Ransom Papers, Vanderbilt University Archives; Ransom to Allen Tate, January 11, 1952, in Allen Tate Papers, Firestone Library, Princeton University.
2. Christopher Dawson, the English writer associated with the Catholic Distributist movement of social reform in the 1930s and whom Eliot credits in the preface to *Notes Towards the Definition of Culture* (New York, 1949) for several of the ideas therein, had also been a close colleague of Ransom's during his English sojourn in

to Ransom, is a poet whom "naturalistic thinkers" ought to find congenial (*SE*, 284–85). And in the same year, Ransom sent a letter to the New York publisher Alfred A. Knopf that indicated his own commitment to the sentiments he was attributing to Stevens:

> I have the extremest liking for his verse, and it is a fact that I think it is valuable not only for its poetic quality but for its ideas: for me he is arguing on behalf of a secular culture based on Nobility, and I think that is the best culture that we are going to have, and a practicable one at the same time; though his critics have never mentioned this, it is very plain if one reads the poems, and it will become plainer, indeed it will become compulsive, when the Collected Poems are issued all in one volume.[3]

But whereas Stevens—with whose philosophical position Ransom once said he totally agreed—and Eliot had written *notes* on "a Supreme Fiction" and on culture respectively, Ransom had in a sense attempted more. His early poetry, his unorthodox book defending what he thought was orthodoxy, and his many essays on aesthetics, though frequently repetitive, provide a much more extensive treatment of his ideas than Stevens' and Eliot's poetic and prose writings explicitly offer about theirs.

Ransom's further development in this general direction during the 1950s and 1960s can be seen, first, in those essays in which he is mainly concerned with expounding his own position and, second, in a series of important writings in which he reexamines his attitude toward the major poets that have interested him throughout his long lifetime—Milton, Wordsworth, Hardy, Stevens, and finally, of course, Eliot. This approach serves to highlight a particular continuity in Ransom's thought that might otherwise pass relatively unnoticed amidst what has too often seemed to be no more than a random assortment of individual essays composed for a variety of literary occasions.

1931 when they sometimes engaged in rather heated argument on religion and economics. See Young, *Gentleman in a Dustcoat*, 244.

3. Ransom, quoted in Milton J. Bates's *Wallace Stevens: A Mythology of Self* (Berkeley, 1985), 266. When Herbert Weinstock suggested using Ransom's comment for publicity, Stevens admitted that it had "[hit] the bull's eye" but that he did not want to be classed with the secular humanists or social humanitarians, "the healers who speak (and take up collections) on Sundays in parlors at the Waldorf, and so on." Although this was not at all what Ransom had in mind, he understood Stevens' explanation to him that "The trouble is that once one is strongly defined, no other definition is ever possible, in spite of daily change" (267). The same, of course, might be said about the classification that Ransom himself has tended to receive from literary critics—sympathetic and otherwise.

By the early 1950s, in both the United States and Great Britain, the most extreme claims of positivistic philosophy had been under siege for several years, so that many of its most ardent proponents were at least aware of the inadequacies of their formulations and were busily attempting to revise them in order to correct their in-advertent—though frequently arrogant—errors. And W. V. O. Quine's attack on the dogmas of empiricism, Wittgenstein's theory of self-regulating "language games," and J. L. Austin's meticulous analyses of a variety of ordinary "speech acts," however much these philosophers may have differed from one another, were all attempts at reaccommodating certain forms of linguistic behavior that had been all too easily dismissed by the positivists one or two decades earlier. Although he does not mention any of these au-thors by name (and would certainly have argued with much of what they claimed), Ransom must have known that such philo-sophical developments were in the air, and they must have been congenial to him since, like Dewey, he had always been rather skeptical of an excessively confident positivism that left no room for the claims of the aesthetic sensibility. Nevertheless, "the cold and dull side of mid-century" saw him continuing to be sympa-thetic toward positivism's less aggressive companion, naturalism, and still trying to find a place for poetry within its theoretical framework.[4] But perhaps he felt that the period was dull partly be-cause he himself was no longer engaged in his intellectual struggles with quite the same passion that had absorbed him during the 1930s and 1940s. One could look on the early 1930s, for example, as the time when, on behalf of an aesthetic "religion"—in Ransom's peculiar, nonescapist understanding of "aesthetic"—he had been combating the excessive claims of science, and on the 1940s as the time when he had been taken up with a defense of poetry against the aggressive religionists and metaphysicians. By the 1950s and 1960s, then, having already achieved a certain acceptance for some of his views and at a time when poetry was thriving at least within the universities, Ransom was more inclined simply to state his case and let his readers make of it what they would.

Moreover, whatever his personal view may have been, Ransom was not drawn toward those dramatic declarations of unbelief com-mon among certain of the European existentialists whose works

4. Ransom, "The Poems of T. S. Eliot: A Perspective," 16.

were appearing at the time in America. Ransom had himself published some of the first general accounts of the movement in the
pages of the *Kenyon Review*, and the essays there by Marjorie Grene
and Walter Kaufmann would later become standard introductory
texts. Martin Buber's presentation of religious revelation as an I-
Thou encounter—rather than a series of dogmatic propositions re-
quiring merely intellectual assent—had appeared in the journal as
early as 1942. Although Ransom was to mention the existentialists
from time to time and certainly saw their "alienation" as akin to his
own "disaffection," for the most part he was skeptical of their philosophy. He was aware that it was a revolt against Hegel's all-
embracing idealism and had on one occasion even used Gabriel
Marcel's criticisms of a technical view of the world to support his
own argument on behalf of "precious objects," but in spite of the
interest he shared with these philosophers in regard to the concrete and the particular, he seems to have been less sympathetic
with their stress on the passionate subjectivity of the individual.
Such an attitude was not congenial to his own more naturalistic
sensibility. His assistant editor at the *Kenyon Review*, Philip Blair
Rice, had even argued in an essay that Ransom later anthologized
that much of what was useful in existentialist philosophy—particularly the emphasis on immediate experience—was already
available in more lucid and balanced form in the writings of the
major American pragmatist philosophers.[5]

Just how far Ransom had advanced in a thoroughly naturalistic—
and nonexistentialist—direction is readily apparent from his comments on Dostoyevsky's *The Possessed* in "The Understanding of
Fiction," an essay written about a topic on which he normally remained silent but which, characteristically, he felt was becoming
more and more important as the century progressed. Indeed, it
had been almost twenty years since he had acknowledged regret-
fully that the tense of poetry was the past and that in the present
age "those parts [of the mind] which are not active in prose are
thoroughly suppressed, and can hardly break through and exercise themselves" (*WB*, 237). At all events, in Dostoyevsky's novel,
the character Kirillov is driven by the realization of his lack of reli-

5. John Crowe Ransom, "The Understanding of Fiction," *Kenyon Review*, XII
(Spring, 1950), 191; Philip Blair Rice, "Existentialism and the Self," in John Crowe
Ransom (ed.), *The Kenyon Critics* (New York, 1951), 200–24.

gious belief to kill himself. Ransom's simple comment on the incident is that the idea of God has, since that novel was written, been modified by scientific empiricism and has lost its "desperate compulsion," so that a Western man "could not nowadays easily get himself into the mortal dilemma of Kirillov."[6]

"Two fateful ideas figure specially with the characters of Dostoyevsky," Ransom notes, "God, and the revolution." But whereas in Dostoyevsky's view socialism is a secular religion, the "atheist substitute for God," Ransom's preference is not for one over the other because he sees the problems in both. While, for example, "Marx's idea on its constructive side, where it looks forward to the society of the blest which by a remarkable logical necessity must follow hard upon the [political] crisis, might have for analogue the apocalyptic vision of a Hebrew prophet, or an early Christian," what is important is that neither Marxism nor Christianity has survived the empirical and pragmatic test of time: the Russian revolution "has not been anything like its promise," and "the theological impulse" has come "to be finally and surely affected" by the advances of science.[7]

Nevertheless, Ransom asserts, there must be "an elemental character in the psyche which sets off spontaneously those strange behaviors [quests for religious or secular utopias]" since their existence has been confirmed again and again and, indeed, Freud has examined them scientifically. It is the same impulses, Ransom argues, that give rise to poetry. Thus—following the lines he had adopted in "The Inorganic Muses"—he is no longer troubled when it is pointed out to him that some poetic statements might be "nonsense." Certain types of "nonsense" are valid because in them a "use-object" is elevated into a "concrete object" for contemplation and the satisfaction of the affections (213). But he emphasizes once again that such elevations must be grounded in the natural constitution of man, a fact that modern thinkers have brought to one's acute awareness: "They must be somewhat reckless persons who think no public good is done by the philosophical naturalist, the logical positivist, the Freudian psychologist; as well as by the alienated artist who impeaches so openly the exhaustion of the historic arts, religions, manners, all of them transcendental formations

6. Ransom, "The Understanding of Fiction," 207–208.
7. Ibid., 206, 207.

of our culture." What is happening in general, Ransom thinks, is that the specific forms of the present culture are changing either because they have grown too peremptory—a reference, surely, to the religionists—or because they have lost their vitality. New forms, however, will be created by the "common affections," and so "we do not require a host of transcendental impulses" for this enterprise.[8]

Given this willingness on Ransom's part to surrender a transcendental account of the origins of even the higher impulses of man in favor of a more naturalistic explanation, it might seem incongruous that it was at this time also that he was to make his most frequent and extensive references to the transcendentalist philosophers par excellence, Kant and Hegel. But Kant's importance for Ransom had never really been in doubt, since it was this philosopher who had been the first to stake out a separate realm for art (as opposed to science and morals) with his *Critique of Judgment*. What is significant about Ransom's comments in the 1950s is that the nuances of his Kantian sympathies are fully revealed, nuances indicating that he read Kant in the British empiricist tradition—"We must approve of his [Kant's] philosophical background. It was a British philosopher [Hume] who woke him from his 'dogmatic slumber,' and conditioned him to the sort of intellectual scruple with which an empirical thinker faces the facts of life and of nature." But Ransom's comments also suggest that he was prepared to concede that present-day culture might require "a far more radical and imaginative psychology and anthropology than existed in Kant's time" (*SE*, 293, 290).

More importantly, Ransom prefers Kant to Hegel because Kant refused to subsume the "tissue of events whose effects are massive and intricate beyond the grasp of the understanding" under some overarching theory of ideal rationality (*SE*, 294). In other words, Kant was more attuned to the inexhaustible richness and plurality of nature than was a synthesizing Hegel. For Ransom, Hegel's "Concrete Universal" formulation—which he had temporarily embraced in *God Without Thunder*, though even then criticizing subsequent Hegelians for emphasizing one element to the detriment of the other—has been found not to work, and it is to Kant that he

---

8. *Ibid.*, 213, 217–18.

turns for a suitable example of why this is so: "In a garden the foliage or the blossoms of the plants will answer insofar as the general profile is concerned to the gardener's geometrical Universal, yet their configuration in its profuse detail is much too intricate . . . and implies energies not used up by the Universal" (*SE*, 294). Richard Rorty's criticisms of Dewey's lingering Kantianism can be applied almost word for word to Ransom also, while Dewey's tentative Hegelianism, which Rorty praises, is precisely what Ransom criticizes in his favorite pragmatist thinker. Rorty writes:

> Philosophy, for Kant, as it had been for Aristotle, was a matter of drawing boundaries to keep scientific inquiry from interfering with morals, the aesthetic from interfering with the scientific, and so on. For Hegel, on the other hand, Newtonian physics, the contrite consciousness, and the delight in landscape gardens were brief episodes in the development of the spirit: stepping-stones on the way to a culture that would encompass all of these without dividing them from one another. For Dewey, the quests for truth, for moral virtue, and for aesthetic bliss are seen as distinct and potentially competing activities only if one thinks of truth as "accuracy of representation," of moral virtue as purity of heart, and of beauty as "purposiveness without purpose." He did not question the accuracy of Kant's description of the eighteenth century's ways of thinking of these things, but with Hegel, he questioned the necessity of staying in the eighteenth century.[9]

Ransom consistently opposed the idea that "the delight in landscape gardens" was merely a "brief episode in the development of the spirit."

Finally, however, in spite of his keen admiration for Kant, Ransom makes a clear distinction between the German philosopher's faith and his own kind of piety: "The faith of Kant the philosopher was formed on intellectual grounds, it was other-worldly yet of extreme Protestant severity, *quite declining to let the imagination of this world give it form"*; on the other hand, the poet's faith or piety "is that this is 'the best of all possible worlds'; inasmuch as *it is not possible for imagination to acquaint us with any other world"* (*SE*, 303–304, my emphasis). Ransom had no scruple about disregarding Kant and making a radical adaptation of Leibniz (or indeed of any other philosopher) whenever his naturalistic bent required it.

What Ransom seems most aware of in his essays at this time is that the philosophers he had once depended on (and still relies on

9. Rorty, "Dewey's Metaphysics," in *Consequences of Pragmatism*, 86.

to some extent) for his aesthetic theories need to be supplemented with more recent scientific findings. In the case of Aristotle, for example, Ransom is troubled that this philosopher's followers at the University of Chicago (R. S. Crane and his associates—not those philosophers connected with the *International Encyclopedia of Unified Science*), frustrated "when their own speculations [on aesthetics] were not exactly coming through on schedule," had turned to the "authority" of an ancient thinker (*SE*, 268). Ransom claims that he too might have done so at one time but that he has since found Aristotle lacking in many important areas: "If I try to force from him some pronouncement by implication, the starch starts going out of the whole business; clearly this is not the way to proceed in it." His conclusion, therefore, is that "we still have to search out the mysteries as they offer themselves, and from where we stand" (*SE*, 270).

When, therefore, Ransom finally comes to present the results of his own searching out of the mysteries, he agrees with Kant that God is simply unknown, but then rejects the religious faith for which Kant claimed to have left room, and rejects even more strongly Hegel's "grave divergence from philosophical propriety" in asserting that "he knew God and His goodness, though others might not." Since, according to Ransom, a person's theological beliefs can only derive from his experience in this world, they can tell him nothing about some future state; moreover, the painful truth is that he lives in a universe where there is no obvious harmony between the experienced indifference of nature and the supposed concern of a divine providence. Thus Ransom's statement of his own secular "faith" is that "this is 'the best of all possible worlds.' . . . It is a horrid as well as a beautiful world, but without the horror we should never focus the beauty; without death there would be no relish for life; without danger, no courage; without savagery, no gentleness; and without the background of our frequent ignominy, no human dignity and pride" (*SE*, 304). Or, in terms of poetry:

> In the poem we have here or there, and in some confused sense all together, nearly every thing we can possibly desire. It is the best of all possible worlds. That is to say, it is erected upon our actual and Leibnitzian world as its base, and there is no other kind of world to which we can conceivably make our human adaptation without mutilating our nature. Of course, it is not really possible, inasmuch as we have

idealized it and improved it a little by our art. But when we settle down into that grim realization, we are beyond the help of any poems at all.[10]

Variants of this formula can be found scattered throughout Ransom's essays and speeches of the 1950s and 1960s. In a 1964 talk on Theodore Roethke's poem "In a Dark Time," for example, Ransom refers to the idea of immortality as "specious" and claims that if one insists on seeing the theological credentials of a poet, they would reduce to "some wide and windy proclamation like this: How excellently is the world made, that death should have been provided in order to achieve life: do we not faithfully testify to the best of all possible worlds?" He explains Roethke's theistic images as being "metaphysical and factitious only as physical entities invented in order to clear up the mysterious structure of the mind." In his tribute to Allen Tate, who had become a Roman Catholic in 1950, Ransom indicates that they have rather different views on the modern world. But now, since the Roman church, the "strictest of the Christian bodies in asserting its religious authority," has come to terms with political power, modern science, and even ancient paganism—the kind of alliance that he had condemned in *God Without Thunder*—his own faith does not appear to him to be so heretical after all: "I come back to what I was saying earlier, and confess that my regular piety is that of a pagan, or a primitive, and that my regular theology is something improvised to suit the literary occasion." Even when he confesses in 1965 that he is "neither capable nor desirous of abandoning the instruction I received in my father's parsonage," he is simply talking about "the idea of the God who created out of chaos a slowly evolving universe, coming to its highest climax in the mind and brain of man," an idea that he finds to be the best "hypothesis" available.[11]

10. Ransom, "The Concrete Universal," in *Beating the Bushes*, 173, and "Humanism at Chicago," in *Poems and Essays*, 101.
11. John Crowe Ransom, "On Theodore Roethke's 'In a Dark Time,'" in Anthony Ostroff (ed.), *The Contemporary Poet as Artist and Critic* (Boston, 1964), 30, 34; Ransom, "In Amicitia," *Sewanee Review*, LXVII (Fall, 1959), 535–36, 538; Ransom, "Theory of Poetic Form," in William J. Handy (ed.), *A Symposium on Formalist Criticism* (Austin, 1965), 17. In notes made for a 1967 talk (never delivered) at Denison University, Ohio, on "The Religion of the Poets," Ransom considers sympathetically and in some detail a passage from Bertrand Russell's *Autobiography* which argues that religion diminishes our appreciation of the beauties of this world. Later on, in a series of numbered jottings, Ransom questions whether he himself might not be a Deist since he tends to believe in a Creator, though not in a special Providence, and cer-

The nature of Ransom's faith appears in even more prominent relief in his rereadings of those major poets with whom he had been especially preoccupied over the years. Indeed, he seems at times to have chosen to write new essays on Milton, Wordsworth, Hardy, Stevens, and Eliot that he might examine, not so much his position in relation to theirs—though that is sometimes his overt strategy—but rather theirs in relation to his, whether by way of agreement or disagreement with it. The title alone of his essay on Milton, for example, suggests how much he had changed since the 1930s. "The Idea of a Literary Anthropologist and What He Might Say of the *Paradise Lost* of Milton" is important not only because in it Ransom claims to be taking a "theological approach," albeit his "qualifications are most irregular," but also because his attitude toward Milton therein is in marked contrast to that which he had held almost thirty years earlier (*SE*, 327). He now finds himself disagreeing with Milton's, and the Bible's, account of the expulsion from Eden insofar as it implies that the pursuit of knowledge is a bad thing. He has revised his opinion from the days when he was "an uncritical Milton scholar, though a small one," and wants to stress that "the knowledge which was forbidden [to Adam and Eve] on theological grounds is the knowledge which means to improve" (*SE*, 331). New theologies will have to be formed, therefore, and presumably they will be less authoritarian than the old ones.

In this essay Ransom takes a position that he had attacked in *God Without Thunder*. He claims that "the new theological notions are tacit" and that "it may make unnecessary trouble if they are not" (*SE*, 334). The new theologians would rewrite the Genesis story so that the expulsion would appear as a good thing, for it is in the real world, and not in the "dull sheltered Garden," that man discovers his true happiness. It is necessary for man to experience pain and death in order to come into awareness of the beauties of transient life. And he must also have a keen wit "to see the knowledge of the world's secrets and put them to work"—science. Ransom concludes with a statement that echoes that given in "The Understanding of Fiction": now "we have a new economy," and are "painfully arriving at a new total culture" and "doubtless a new theology, tacit and private mostly, to justify it" (*SE*, 335–36).

---

tainly not in the hope of an afterlife (John Crowe Ransom Papers, Vanderbilt University Archives).

Ransom's naturalistic sensibility is even more evident in "William Wordsworth: Notes Toward an Understanding of Poetry," published in 1950. In *The New Criticism*, he had agreed with Empson's judgment that the well-known "religious" passage in "Tintern Abbey" that begins "For I have learnt / To look on nature" was the work of a poet "holding muddled opinions" rather than displaying a complex mind (*NC*, 119). He repeats that criticism in this essay, noting that the passage's eloquence is "that of a kind of straining, muddled Protestant theologism" (*SE*, 261). But he now wants to offer "a modern or post-Wordsworthian fable," the parts of which, he explains, may be found scattered (though undeveloped) throughout Dewey's philosophical writings. According to this fable, man finds himself born into a universe that is indifferent to him but in which aesthetic experience enables him to overcome that indifference and thus return "to nature, his mother, yet in his own character and without suffering death"(*SE*, 259). Ransom stresses the fact that Wordsworth would not have accepted the first part of the fable (the notion of the world being indifferent to man), though the second is very much in harmony with that poet's inheritance from the German idealist philosophers and from Coleridge (presumably when their works are given a pantheistic reading).

Ransom's main concern in such a context, then, is to show that Wordsworth was simply wrong in his interpretation of his earliest experiences. In a number of critical comments on *The Prelude*, he notes with regret that "a heavy overlay of religious experience is added to the spontaneous joy of the boy's simple affections. A more or less uniform religious doctrine is adhered to throughout the poem, and brought to consciousness within the boy's response almost every time before the poet will leave him alone." Although Ransom recognizes that Wordsworth is following the teachings of the German mystic Jakob Boehme, he nevertheless objects:

> Now I should not wish to scorn a cosmic compassion which resorts by such tricks, such very human tricks, to these philanthropic aggressions. But in the name of David Hartley, who is another of Wordsworth's heroes, I suggest that pragmatically, psychologically, it is more usual for us to regard the cosmic constructs of religion as fashioned afterwards, and indeed upon the base of those spontaneous affective responses which people make to nature; so that in the ordering which Wordsworth authorizes, the cart is before the horse. We have a mystical experience which precedes its own empirical technique.   (*SE*, 260)

In siding with Hartley over Boehme, Ransom is declaring his own preference for the empirical over the mystical approach to reality. Thus, in spite of the fact that *The Prelude* is undoubtedly a religious poem, he is distressed that Wordsworth has "read back into the boy's mind some of the mature configurations of his own." Ransom adds significantly: "And I think we may prefer to take our poetry as an experience which is local, and plural, rather than cosmic, and one. It will still give the quick joy, and the instant sense of community with the natural objects, and we can go a long way on that" (*SE*, 261). Ransom is once again opposing an idealism in which the objects of nature all too readily point beyond themselves to some absolute and recommending instead a genuine naturalism that delights in the sheer density of the material world.

Ransom is pleased therefore that "Ode on Intimations of Immortality" [*sic*]—which he elsewhere infelicitously but pointedly retitles "Intimations of Goodness in the Body of This World" (*SE*, 317)—suggests that even Wordsworth himself had misgivings about the religious insights he imposed upon the child. Objecting again to Wordsworth's subsequent "laborious dogma" and arguing that "natural piety" is better explained by Hartley than by Boehme, Ransom draws attention to the heart of the problem: "In that poem [*The Prelude*] he had read off to his adult readers the intuitive religiousness of the child as if it were a universal and exemplary experience. But what if the adult mind cannot have this experience? Wordsworth came to the melancholy conviction that it lacked the power. And what if the child's mind lacked it too, if Wordsworth in the excess of his prodigious memory had given it more power than it had had? I think that we will imagine that his question harrowed the poet" (*SE*, 265). What one is left with, then, in *The Prelude*, according to Ransom, "is a very full account of Wordsworth's religious experience itself at a certain period, however it may have been achieved." Meanwhile, Ransom himself prefers the shorter poems: "They are the fundamental earth, or they are the foundation stones, upon which if there is to be a religious edifice it must rise" (*SE*, 266). The tone of this observation scarcely inspires confidence that Ransom himself had much interest or belief in the construction of such an edifice.

It was in Thomas Hardy, more than in any other writer, that Ransom found intellectual and emotional kinship. Hardy, having grown up in an environment not altogether unlike Ransom's, expressed religious opinions and doubts that were also similar to his. The last of Ransom's many essays on this poet, first read as a paper at Northwestern University and subsequently developed for the introduction to a selection of Hardy's poems brought out by Macmillan in 1961, depicts him as a modern naturalist wanting to find his God. Hardy's poetic endeavor was the work of "a metaphysical imagination, in the service of a theological passion," and in poetry he could indulge in speculation in a way that was not possible in his novels. Thus Ransom goes on to note that while the rhythm of "The Subalterns" (an old favorite) derives from church hymns, when one comes to its meaning, "which is our major preoccupation," one finds that it is quite heretical and unacceptable to any of the churches. What the poem suggests to Ransom is that Hardy exemplifies "the Classical Spirit." From his description of this classical spirit—a description that is couched at several places in phrases that he had earlier applied to himself—one can see that it is also very much his own:

> Its faith is in a created world in which our species can manage very well because we are adapted biologically to it, and by acting rationally become better and better adapted. The Subalterns such as we can distinguish must execute its laws, but they are at least as beneficent as they are harsh. Though the final outcome for individual man is death, he has a good chance to realize his share of happiness; and this for him, peculiarly among the created forms of life, is conscious and thrilling precisely because of his sense of the perils by which it is invested. He feels that the world is good, perhaps that it is the best of all possible worlds, as the religious philosopher said; and when he thinks of its creator he would be theologically of some Deistic persuasion.[12]

Continuing in this latently autobiographical vein, Ransom suggests that exposure to the arguments of Darwin's *Origin of Species* and listening to the proponents of the higher criticism of the Bible must have precipitated Hardy's crisis of faith. Hardy's first efforts in literature may have been undertaken "to confirm and publish his own theological speculations." Then, displaying more than a hint of nostalgia for his own lost childhood beliefs, Ransom muses:

> We think of him [Hardy] wishing he might return to the religious community of his boyhood, to the old faith, and the physical Church and its hymns. He was deterred, as many another naturalist must be more or

12. Ransom (ed.), *Selected Poems of Thomas Hardy*, ix, xiv–xv, xx.

less, by his conscientious objection to reciting the belief that God interposes in the execution of the natural laws by the faithful Subalterns. But he had the Spirit of Irony to mitigate his distress. The ironic disposition of evil may look to us like an interim arrangement, while he was collecting his wits and gathering his courage again; and so it was. Yet there is a massive but naughty pleasure in one's indecision when the choice is between two conflicting allegiances so momentous as Science and Faith, and naturally it can be prolonged. If deprived by some compunction of this refuge he would have had to embrace Science and go without Faith. But meanwhile it is as if he were holding in abeyance the processes of nature while he gave time to some transcendent order to assert itself. We understand the sequel; irony became his rule.

Irony, however, was *not* (as the comment from Donald Davie quoted earlier shows) quite Hardy's "rule" but more that of Housman—and of Ransom, whose essay again is as much autobiographical as it is about its declared subject. Of course, Ransom's general approach is not without validity, for as he remarks at the end of the essay, far from being unique to the late Victorians, the search for the unknown God "may be attributed with some confidence to almost any serious poet." [13]

The emphasis on naturalism and on a "this-worldly"—as opposed to supernatural—faith is tempered in the Hardy essay by a straining wistfulness for lost certainties, as if Ransom in his old age desired to return to the spiritual comfort of his own remote past in a Tennessee parsonage. But it is no more than tempered, for he still finds himself philosophically unable to profess any form of Christian orthodoxy. This fact is evident in his extended commentary on Wallace Stevens' career in "The Planetary Poet," an essay published in 1964 that is also very much shaped by the trajectory of his own religious progress. Here he calls Stevens a philosophical poet and a "priest-like poet, who labored long in finding his credo." Stevens was a "very good Kantian," though he probably

13. *Ibid.*, xxxii, xxiv, xxxii. When, during these last years, Ransom returned to his published poems in order to revise some of them for a new selected edition, he changed the title of "Conrad in Twilight" to "Master's in the Garden Again" with a shift of reference from Joseph Conrad to Thomas Hardy. The new reference is to a poem Hardy wrote in 1917, "The Master and the Leaves," at a time when he "was too dispirited by the World War, and perhaps too tired, to spend himself reiterating his old defiance against the Power that knows no special providence for Its creatures." The tone of Ransom's revised poem is lighthearted, however, because—significantly—there is "no chance of hurting, nor of reaching, nor even of finding the awful Power" (John Crowe Ransom, "On 'Master's in the Garden Again,'" in Ostroff [ed.], *The Contemporary Poet as Artist and Critic*, 136, 139).

did not read the philosopher, "bringing his own thought into a Kantian order without the benefit of Kant or the pain of Kant's formidable jargon." Priestlike, he shared a bond "with professional poets, who were concerned like himself with the definition of their faith."[14] Presumably, Ransom—insofar as he too was a poet and the son of a Methodist minister, though he had not received the "gift"—considered himself to be a member of this group.

According to Ransom, Stevens "did not like the idea of the resurrection of the body," preferring instead "the finality of death," a preference evidenced most strongly in "The Emperor of Ice-Cream." Quoting from "Sunday Morning" as the fullest of Stevens' poems about death, Ransom concurs with the notion that without religious belief (or, at least, belief in an afterlife)

> The sky will be much friendlier then than now,
> A part of labor and a part of pain,
> And next in glory to enduring love,
> Not this dividing and indifferent blue.

Stevens' idea here is hardly very different from the one Ransom himself had expressed much less gracefully in "Sunset" in 1916. Stevens' proper song, then, from which he sometimes strayed, "is of the visible glories of his own world."[15]

Ransom provides an interesting explanation for what he discerns as Stevens' antipathy toward the churches and priests: "[If] we should have to define his philosophical views on the whole, he would be a philosophical naturalist, perhaps a logical positivist; yet well acquainted as a healthy natural man with a moral imperative and willing to let it manage for itself. Finally, he did not approve the supernatural sanctions which the churches asserted, that is, the heaven or hell hereafter, though with increasing latitude of conviction." Ransom goes on to admit that Stevens later abandoned his feud with the churches, and quotes from Stevens' poem on Santayana, "To an Old Philosopher in Rome," in support of this: "On the threshold of heaven, the figures in the street / Become the figures of heaven." But he nevertheless adds the caution that "the faith of Stevens is an aesthetic faith, not a theological faith."[16]

Again and again, Ransom superimposes his own version of Kantianism on Stevens, commending this philosophy as against a

14. John Crowe Ransom, "The Planetary Poet," *Kenyon Review*, XXVI (Winter, 1964), 235.

15. *Ibid.*, 244, 252.

16. *Ibid.*, 254, 258.

Hegelianism in which "the arts and their deficiencies would be outmoded." *The Phenomenon of Man* "by the priest Pierre Teilhard de Chardin" is offered in passing as a recent example of such Hegelianism and is described in a way that would surely have surprised its author as "the most forbidding image of man's future on this planet." The autobiographical note in one of his final comments on Stevens "in the middle of his seventies"—which was also Ransom's age when he was writing the essay—is especially revealing: in Stevens one now finds "a tranquillity toward the people and places and faiths he had once scorned, as if now he conceded them their equal right to be." Indeed, Ransom tends to underline the self-referentiality of his remarks when he admits that they are "beside the point" of the essay's topic and that Stevens himself would have "detested" them.[17]

The best instance of Ransom's own "tranquillity toward the people and places and faiths he had once scorned" is to be found, as one might expect, in his later treatment of T. S. Eliot, "the lion in [Ransom's] path," as Tate once described him. Eliot's progress had been from "secularism back to the faith," while Ransom's had gone in the opposite direction (*WB*, 355). Having rejected *The Waste Land* first of all because of its prosody and formlessness, Ransom found that by the time he had caught up in that respect, "a shift of ideas had come over me, to hinder even a belated appreciation." He explains:

> *The Waste Land* . . . began to seem to me too sweeping in its representation of the secular horrors; an exhibit of an age where all the pictures were unsavory. I was suspicious about the uniformity of these appearances, and that was at the time when I was questioning the evidences which had led to my own personal set against the age. But the long and short of it comes to this, that I could not find the certain reasons for thinking the modern society was destitute of its normal humanity, and in the midst of all the confusion I began to have hopes for it, even on its own terms.[18]

That remark was written in 1952 when Ransom thought that Eliot was at last moving in the same direction as himself. By 1968, in his postscript to a new edition of *The World's Body*, he was ready to take an even more generous view of Eliot and to suggest that their respective paths might not have been that dissimilar after all.

At the beginning of his literary career, according to Ransom,

17. *Ibid.*, 259, 263, 254.
18. Ransom, "The Poems of T. S. Eliot: A Perspective," 16.

"Eliot was like many another young man who had lost his faith and was trying to recover it," so that "this is the point of the argument which determines the text in the first place" (*WB*, 353). It soon becomes clear, however, that the nub of the issue for Ransom is how one is to interpret those "still moments" that occur under various names in several of Eliot's poems, culminating in *Four Quartets*. He had interpreted their appearance in the earlier verse from an aesthetic point of view:

> I had kept a close watch over Eliot's "still moments," and for me it was sufficient if one of them presented a natural moment having an aesthetic confirmation; and in my amateur's philosophy I had said to myself that such a moment seemed to bring us into the presence of the unknown God who gave us the sense of beauty and caused beauty to appear in his creation, establishing at least a moment of communion. Beauty ranked even above morality, and was our highest natural faculty. If I half felt these impressions, I was convinced by the aesthetic of Kant, which I took, and take, to be on the highest human authority. For Wordsworth in his early years, the natural revelations served as the cardinal point of faith.   (*WB*, 363)

But, reading *Ash-Wednesday*, Ransom found himself sorely "discomfited" when he encountered there a special "still moment" of prayer that is made in darkness and alone. Nevertheless, because this moment does not lead Eliot to "spurn" the "still moments" in which beauty is perceived, and because its supremacy occurs only two or three times, Ransom is willing to forgo criticism of it.

When he encounters such a moment again in *Four Quartets* as "the intersection of the timeless with time," however, acknowledging that Eliot himself would not have done so, Ransom turns to the philosophy of Bergson for its justification. Bergson "demonstrated experimentally that there were many occasions when distinct and remembered moments of consciousness in the psyche did not leave any tracks whatever within the physiology of the brain" (*WB*, 365). Ransom is therefore willing to allow that he had been burdening himself with "unnecessary mystification" concerning the authenticity of Eliot's moments; a true empiricist (though the empirical value of Bergson's reasoning remains highly questionable), he requires a naturalistic explanation before he can accept the reported experience, and even then he remains somewhat hesitant as to its true content, "the lift of the soul in the vertical direction, where the God is generally assumed to have his residence" (*WB*, 366).

In the end, Ransom feels compelled by "an uneasy tic in my conscience" to "sound a certain dissenting note" as to Eliot's faith, though he thinks now that Eliot (whose own faith as expressed in *The Waste Land* was also not orthodox) might have approved of his position. Ransom then gives the fullest account of his religious beliefs:

> I have never imposed my own faith on anybody particularly, but for this occasion I do not mind calling it Unitarian. I had backslid from my father's faith to that position even before I came upon Kant the Transcendentalist, who did not dare to make images of the Unknown God. And that is exactly the position which nowadays even the clergy of most churches, including the Roman Catholic, have found themselves desperately studying and frequently accepting. Wherever Christ is mentioned, not as the great Saint or Prophet but as a junior member of the godhead, it is because he promised to his followers that immortality which Kant had named as the third of the three aspirations of the Pure Reason—the soul itself—even though it is the least capable of logical demonstration. And I think that most of the communicants, and many of the clergy itself, have little interest in that article of faith; but do not go about advertising their dissidence because they know that every now and then they will have to attend a service for the dead, where there will be a bereaved family who may find a vicarious comfort in the Promise read by the officiating clergy. (*WB*, 376–77)

When one examines this apparent profession of faith, one is struck by how much of it is devoted to a reaffirmation of those criticisms of religious belief that Ransom had offered in *God Without Thunder* almost forty years earlier. Not only does God remain completely unknown, but the clergy of the Roman church are "desperately" studying the situation and even admitting its truth. It is necessary to proclaim Christ a "junior member of the godhead"—though he is really only a prophet—merely because people need to be consoled now and then in regard to the afterlife that he promised and that is quite implausible anyway. Ransom's "faith" at this late date, therefore, reduces to what it had always been: a contented agnosticism that generally affirmed no more than experience allowed. It was wishful thinking for Ransom to suggest that Eliot's beliefs might not be so very different from his after all, and indeed he sensibly cautioned himself that he would have to wait "to ask some of Eliot's closest friends" about the matter (*WB*, 378).

Following his retirement from teaching and from editorship of the *Kenyon Review* in 1959, Ransom remained active in the academic world, writing new essays, planning a revision of his poems, lecturing, and collecting those belated honors and recognitions that usually grace the closing years of a distinguished literary career. He also began to suffer from a variety of recurring ailments that gradually led him into long periods of withdrawal and silence. Several years before this happened, on his seventy-fifth birthday in 1963, Ransom spoke of himself in the third person thus: "If he lives out his three score and ten (as this poet did) he will come into the peace which accompanies the sense of having achieved all the wisdom that was available for him, and he will be happy to subside, happy but used up, into the annihilation of death." [19] Unlike Wallace Stevens, Ransom did not finally return to the solace of formal religious belief; rather, his life itself confirmed the secular faith he had defined and argued for in his writings. [20] It was perhaps slightly ironic, therefore, that though his passing in July, 1974, was marked by no religious rite, the memorial service at the Kenyon College chapel the following November included lines from John Masefield that were hardly appropriate to the character of the man they were meant to honor:

> Sing, creatures, sing; the dust
> That lives by lure and lust
> Is kindled by the thrust
> Of life undying.

On the other hand, Robert Penn Warren, in his eulogy, omitting the references customary at a funeral service because neither he nor his old friend believed in them, described Ransom as above all a "domestic poet," a lover of that which was nearest and dearest to him. "But beyond his domestic poetry," Warren went on, "there was, willy-nilly, another range of thought and feeling. There was the philosopher with a profound awareness of the tensions of his age, and an ironist to whom irony was the only antidote for the tragedy of life." [21] One might now want to add that the two roles were intimately connected: Ransom had used his philosophy to explore the fullest range of the domestic world he inhabited and loved, and had not presumed—or thought it realistically possible—to speculate beyond its ample horizons.

19. Young, *Gentleman in a Dustcoat*, 475.

20. Bates, *Wallace Stevens*, 296–97. The significance of Stevens' final conversion to Roman Catholicism, which was not known until quite recently, is still in dispute.

21. Warren's remarks appear in the November 1, 1974, program for Ransom's memorial service, Chalmers Memorial Library Archives, Kenyon College.

Conclusion

John Crowe Ransom's faith was that "'this is the best of all possible worlds'; inasmuch as it is not possible for imagination to acquaint us with any other world." Such was his belief from almost the beginning of his life, and he spent most of his career, on the one hand, seeking out ways in which he could know this world better and, on the other, criticizing those who would distract man from his primary concern by claiming that his true home is elsewhere, whether in a religious or a secular utopia. I would now want to stress the "strong" element in Ransom's agnosticism (a term, incidentally, that necessarily carries with it historical implications of some form of rejection), for his argument is not merely that one does not know anything other than that which one has experienced but that one cannot in principle know such things. He was not, therefore, a covert mystic who allowed for a negative theology of indirect religious affirmation (as might be the case with a philosopher like Heidegger) but rather a proponent of the view that if there is a God—and he seems to have been willing finally to concede the likelihood—such a Being remains totally unknown. Consequently, all those who would lay claim to religious *knowledge*—and Eliot was the prime example for Ransom—are going well beyond the available evidence of experience; in other words, quite literally, their claims are ungrounded.

Yet, of course, Ransom's secular faith had itself emerged from a continuous dialogue with the Christian tradition into which he had been born. That was a condition of his culture, and one that Ransom himself would hardly have regretted. "I ought to say," Wallace Stevens remarked in 1940, "that it is a habit of mind with me to be thinking of some substitute for religion. . . . My trouble, and the trouble of a great many people, is the loss of belief in the sort of God in Whom we were all brought up to believe." So, Robert Penn Warren has observed that Ransom's views theologically "are always colored with a touch of sadness and immense charity of spirit. And toughness of mind. My guess is that John had a religious temperament but was committed to the logical process."[1] Although Ransom was never to become anti-Christian in the manner of Empson, this commitment to logic compelled him to state his philosophical opposition to many of those with whom he was otherwise intellectually quite sympathetic—his father, Eliot, Lowell, Brooks, and even Tate—when they attached themselves to a faith in which he could no longer honestly believe.

Louise Cowan has drawn attention to Ransom's affinity with Mircea Eliade, Carl Jung, and others who might be thought of as "soft" interpreters of man's religious experience in that they have a similar respect for it while not themselves belonging to any particular orthodoxy. But Ransom was really drawn more to the "hard" views of thinkers such as Freud and Russell who were not at all sympathetic with the religious phenomenon. Perhaps this alignment derived from his wish to tackle the problem in the form presented by its most vigorous critics; more likely, however, it arose from his belief that these thinkers had the strongest evidence on their side. Thus, for example, in reflecting on Ransom's interest in the logical-positivist philosophers, it is tempting to see a connection between his thought and that of Wittgenstein, who rejected the narrow positivism of his early *Tractatus Logico-Philosophicus*, in which propositions without a verifiable basis were declared to have no meaning and therefore ought not to be spoken, in favor of a theory of language games in which even theology found a new justification, its terms now coherent and meaningful within its respective system. But Ransom, who apparently was unfamiliar with Wittgenstein's later writings, probably because of their general un-

1. Bates, *Wallace Stevens*, 208; Robert Penn Warren to author, May 5, 1985. It is of interest that in his copy of Simone Weil's *Waiting for God* (New York, 1951), now in the Vanderbilt University Archives, Ransom has marked or underlined several passages in which the Jewish mystic explains her refusal to become a member of the religion she so ardently admires: in one such underlined comment, for example, she states that "Christ likes us to prefer truth to him because, before being Christ, he is truth" (69). T. S. Eliot, who wrote a commendatory preface to one of Weil's books, at the same time cautioned against what he referred to as her "universalist" religious tendency and her excessive independence in matters of belief—characteristics of her temperament that seem to have had special appeal for Ransom.

availability until the 1950s, would most likely have thought that Wittgenstein's ideas justified any kind of language game whatever and in this sense were too pliable to be used in that hard philosophical combat he so often advocated. His real affinity—as evidenced by, among other things, his continuous interest in Dewey from at least 1913 onwards—was with the American pragmatist tradition, which, while receptive to a variety of philosophical approaches, is also critical of the claims of an "aggressive" metaphysics, no matter what quarter it comes from. Of course, as he had observed from the very outset, pragmatism "is such a wide term that few people can endorse all the doctrine which has been put forward under it" (SL, 71).

Several of the issues in philosophy, theology, and literature that preoccupied Ransom—particularly those dealing with the elimination of a metaphysical or transcendental world view—are still being debated. Although the techniques of that debate are more sophisticated than in Ransom's day and perhaps a little tortuous at times, it does not seem likely that an end is in sight. And indeed, one would do well to question whether or not there is any loss in the transition from a culture based on "a host of transcendental impulses" to one without such underpinnings. Certainly the jettisoning of Baudelaire and Rimbaud (to take only a minor example) might cause one to be skeptical about some of the implications of Ransom's apparent program, and there is a lingering suspicion that the character of such a new civilization would be profoundly different from that of the civilization that has gone before.

What seems important for the moment, however, is to emphasize Ransom's secular stance since he is frequently assumed to have held quite a different intellectual position. Thus Edward Said begins his stimulating but occasionally self-righteous book *The World, the Text, and the Critic* with a chapter entitled "Secular Criticism" and ends it with another called "Religious Criticism." Quite predictably, he approves of the former type of criticism and disapproves of the latter type. True criticism for him is "skeptical, secular, reflectively open to its own failings." Religious criticism, on the other hand, is always trying to find an outside authority or to set up a hermetic language and method in order to keep others out. "What one discerns today," he writes, "is religion as the result of exhaustion, consolation, disappointment: its forms in both the theory and practice of criticism are varieties of unthinkability, undecidability, and paradox." This shift in the direction of the more arcane versions of structuralist, poststructuralist, and deconstructionist thought "began four decades ago in the ahistorical, manifestly religious aestheticism of the New Critics."[2] Yet it is interesting that Said, like Ransom, devotes several pages to deploring Eliot's drift toward religion as he moved from "The Love Song of J. Alfred Prufrock" to *Four Quartets*. While, then, Ransom's is certainly a "religious" aestheticism in the Kantian tradition, it is also the case that his *is* a secular criticism of life that is "reflectively open to its own failings" even if, arguably, there are many blindnesses still remaining and even if it differs in important ways from the secular criticism proposed by Said. As Ransom advised the critics at the University of Chicago who looked to Aristotle as an outside authority for the legitimacy of their ventures and a way of escape from the complexities of modern consciousness, "We still have to search out the mysteries as they offer themselves, and from where we stand." In Ransom's world at least, there is simply no atemporal knowledge to be had, and one must learn to live with the uncertainty of a succession of more or less defensible hypotheses.

2. Edward W. Said, *The World, the Text, and the Critic* (Cambridge, Mass., 1983), 26, 291–92. Said also comments on the issue in the preface to the new edition of *Beginnings: Intention and Method* (New York, 1985). Ironically, Giles Gunn finds "sediments of the sacred" in Said's eulogy for Michel Foucault, which was published in 1985 (see Giles Gunn, *The Culture of Criticism and the Criticism of Culture* [New York, 1987], 195).

Bibliography

apRoberts, Ruth. *Arnold and God*. Berkeley, 1983.

Ayer, A. J., ed. *Logical Positivism*. Glencoe, Ill., 1959.

Ayer, A. J., et al. *The Revolution in Philosophy*. London, 1956.

Bates, Milton J. *Wallace Stevens: A Mythology of Self*. Berkeley, 1985.

Blanchard, Brand. "Eliot at Oxford." *Southern Review*, XXI (Autumn, 1985), 889–98.

Brooks, Cleanth. *Modern Poetry and the Tradition*. Chapel Hill, 1970.

Buffington, Robert. *The Equilibrist: A Study of John Crowe Ransom's Poems, 1916–1963*. Nashville, 1967.

Cowan, Louise. *The Fugitive Group: A Literary History*. Baton Rouge, 1959.

——. *The Southern Critics*. Dallas, 1971.

Davidson, Donald. *Southern Writers in the Modern World*. Athens, Ga., 1958.

Davie, Donald. *Thomas Hardy and British Poetry*. New York, 1972.

De Man, Paul. *Allegories of Reading: Figural Language in Rousseau, Nietzsche, Rilke, and Proust*. New Haven, 1979.

Dew, Robb Forman. "Summer's End." *Mississippi Quarterly*, XXX (Winter, 1976–77), 137–53.

Dewey, John. *Experience and Nature*. Chicago, 1925.

——. *The Middle Works, 1899–1924*. Edited by Jo Ann Boydston. Carbondale, Ill., 1976.

Donoghue, Denis. *Ferocious Alphabets*. Boston, 1981.

Durham, Frank. "The Poetry Society of South Carolina's Turbulent Year: Self-Interest, Atheism, and Jean Toomer." *Southern Humanities Review*, V (Winter, 1971), 76–80.

Dykhuizen, George. *The Life and Mind of John Dewey*. Carbondale, Ill., 1973.

Eliot, T. S. *Notes Towards the Definition of Culture*. New York, 1949.

Fekete, John. *The Critical Twilight: Explorations in the Ideology of Anglo-American Literary Theory from Eliot to McLuhan.* London, 1977.

Gelpi, Albert. *A Coherent Splendor: The American Poetic Renaissance, 1910–1950.* New York, 1987.

Gordon, Lyndall. *Eliot's Early Years.* New York, 1977.

Gunn, Giles. *The Culture of Criticism and the Criticism of Culture.* New York, 1987.

Hamilton, Ian. *Robert Lowell: A Biography.* New York, 1982.

Handy, William J. *Kant and the Southern New Critics.* Austin, 1963.

———, ed. *A Symposium on Formalist Criticism.* Austin, 1965.

Hegel, G. W. F. *Phenomenology of Mind.* Translated by J. B. Baillie. New York, 1967.

Hill, Geoffrey. *The Lords of Limit: Essays on Literature and Ideas.* New York, 1984.

James, William. *Pragmatism.* Cambridge, Mass., 1975.

Jarrell, Randall. *Poetry and the Age.* New York, 1953.

Kant, Immanuel. *The Critique of Pure Reason.* Translated by F. Max Müller. London, 1896.

King, Richard H. *A Southern Renaissance: The Cultural Awakening of the American South, 1930–1955.* New York, 1981.

Kirkham, Michael. *The Poetry of Robert Graves.* New York, 1969.

Knoll, Wayne A. "Ransom as Religionist." *Mississippi Quarterly,* XXX (Winter, 1976–77), 111–36.

Krieger, Murray. *The New Apologists for Poetry.* Minneapolis, 1956.

Krikorian, Yervant H., ed. *Naturalism and the Human Spirit.* New York, 1959.

Lindberg-Seyersted, Brita, ed. *Pound / Ford: The Story of a Literary Friendship.* New York, 1982.

Magner, James E., Jr. *John Crowe Ransom: Critical Principles and Preoccupations.* The Hague, 1971.

Manser, Anthony. *Bradley's Logic.* Oxford, 1983.

Maritain, Jacques. "Poetry's Dark Night." *Kenyon Review,* V (Autumn, 1943), 150–60.

Menand, Louis. *Discovering Modernism: T. S. Eliot and His Context.* New York, 1987.

Michaels, Walter Benn. "Philosophy in Kinkanja: Eliot's Pragmatism." *Glyph,* VIII (1981), 170–202.

Miller, J. Hillis. *Poets of Reality.* New York, 1969.

Morris, Charles W. *Writings on the General Theory of Signs.* The Hague, 1971.

Neurath, Otto, Rudolf Carnap, and Charles Morris, eds. *Foundations of the Unity of Science*. Chicago, 1971.

O'Brien, Michael. *The Idea of the American South, 1920–1941*. Baltimore, 1979.

Ogden, C. K., and I. A. Richards. *The Meaning of Meaning*. London, 1949.

Ostroff, Anthony, ed. *The Contemporary Poet as Artist and Critic*. Boston, 1964.

Parsons, Thornton H. *John Crowe Ransom*. New York, 1969.

———. "Ransom and the Poetics of Monastic Ecstasy." *Modern Language Quarterly*, XXVI (December, 1965), 571–84.

Passmore, John. *A Hundred Years of Philosophy*. London, 1968.

Pinsky, Robert. "Hardy, Ransom, Berryman: A 'Curious Air.'" *Agenda*, X (Spring–Summer, 1972), 89–99.

Pratt, William. *The Fugitive Poets: Modern Southern Poetry in Perspective*. New York, 1965.

Ransom, John Crowe. "Alienation a Century Ago." *Kenyon Review*, XV (Spring, 1953), 335–36.

———. *Beating the Bushes: Selected Essays, 1941–1970*. New York, 1972.

———. *Chills and Fever*. New York, 1924.

———. "Emily Dickinson: A Poet Restored." In *Emily Dickinson: A Collection of Critical Essays*, edited by Richard B. Sewall. Englewood Cliffs, 1963.

———. "Gerontion." *Sewanee Review*, LXXIV (Spring, 1966), 389–414.

———. *God Without Thunder: An Unorthodox Defense of Orthodoxy*. New York, 1930; rpr. Hamden, Conn., 1965.

———. *Grace After Meat*. London, 1924.

———. "In Amicitia." *Sewanee Review*, LXVII (Fall, 1959), 528–39.

———. "The Inorganic Muses." *Kenyon Review*, V (Spring, 1943), 278–300.

———, ed. *The Kenyon Critics*. New York, 1951.

———. "Mr. Russell and Mr. Schorer." *Kenyon Review*, IV (Autumn, 1942), 406–407.

———. *The New Criticism*. New York, 1941.

———. "The Planetary Poet." *Kenyon Review*, XXVI (Winter, 1964), 233–64.

———. *Poems About God*. New York, 1919.

———. *Poems and Essays*. New York, 1955.

———. "The Poems of T. S. Eliot: A Perspective." *New Republic,* CXXVII (December 8, 1952), 16–17.

———. "The Question of Justice." *Yale Review,* IV (July, 1915), 684–98.

———. *Selected Essays of John Crowe Ransom.* Edited by Thomas Daniel Young and John Hindle. Baton Rouge, 1984.

———. *Selected Letters of John Crowe Ransom.* Edited by Thomas Daniel Young and George Core. Baton Rouge, 1985.

———. *Selected Poems.* 3rd ed. New York, 1969.

———, ed. *Selected Poems of Thomas Hardy.* New York, 1961.

———. "Strategy for English Studies." *Southern Review,* VI (Autumn, 1940), 226–35.

———. *Two Gentlemen in Bonds.* New York, 1927.

———. "The Understanding of Fiction." *Kenyon Review,* XII (Spring, 1950), 189–218.

———. "Waste Lands." In *T. S. Eliot: The Critical Heritage,* edited by Michael Grant. Vol. I of 2 vols. London, 1982.

———. *The World's Body.* Baton Rouge, 1968.

Rhein, Donna E. *The Handprinted Books of Leonard and Virginia Woolf at the Hogarth Press, 1917–1932.* Ann Arbor, 1985.

Rorty, Richard. *Consequences of Pragmatism.* Minneapolis, 1982.

———. "Genteel Syntheses, Professional Analyses, Transcendentalist Culture." In *Two Centuries of Philosophy in America,* edited by Peter Caws. Totowa, New Jersey, 1980.

Rubin, Louis D. *The Wary Fugitives: Four Poets and the South.* Baton Rouge, 1978.

Russell, Bertrand. "Non-Materialistic Naturalism." *Kenyon Review,* IV (Autumn, 1942), 361–65.

———. *Sceptical Essays.* London, 1956.

Said, Edward W. *Beginnings: Intention and Method.* New York, 1985.

———. *The World, the Text, and the Critic.* Cambridge, Mass., 1983.

Schwartz, Sanford. *The Matrix of Modernism: Pound, Eliot, and Early Twentieth-Century Thought.* Princeton, 1985.

Seymour-Smith, Martin. *Robert Graves: His Life and Work.* New York, 1983.

Singal, Daniel Joseph. *The War Within: From Victorian to Modernist Thought in the South, 1919–1945.* Chapel Hill, 1982.

Spears, Monroe K. *Dionysus and the City: Modernism in Twentieth-Century Poetry.* New York, 1970.

Squires, Radcliffe. *Allen Tate: A Literary Biography.* New York, 1971.

Stevens, Wallace. *Opus Posthumous*. New York, 1957.

Stewart, John L. *The Burden of Time: The Fugitives and Agrarians*. Princeton, 1965.

Szasz, Ferenc Morton. *The Divided Mind of Protestant America, 1880–1930*. University, Ala., 1982.

Tate, Allen. *Collected Poems, 1919–1976*. New York, 1977.

————. *Essays of Four Decades*. Chicago, 1968.

————. *Memoirs and Opinions, 1926–1974*. Chicago, 1975.

Twelve Southerners. *I'll Take My Stand: The South and the Agrarian Tradition*. New York, 1930; rpr. Baton Rouge, 1977.

Warren, Robert Penn. "Notes on the Poetry of John Crowe Ransom at His Eightieth Birthday." *Kenyon Review*, XXX (1968), 319–49.

Wellek, René. *American Criticism, 1900–1950*. New Haven, 1986. Vol. VI of *A History of Modern Criticism, 1750–1950*. 6 vols. to date.

Wollheim, Richard. *F. H. Bradley*. London, 1969.

Young, Thomas Daniel. *Gentleman in a Dustcoat: A Biography of John Crowe Ransom*. Baton Rouge, 1976.

————, ed. *John Crowe Ransom: Critical Essays and a Bibliography*. Baton Rouge, 1968.

Index

Mill, John Stuart, 10
Millikan, R. A., 48
Milton, John: 85; *Lycidas*, xv; *Paradise Lost*, 45, 52–53, 93
Mizener, Arthur, 84
Moore, G. E., 9
Morris, Charles W., 66, 68, 70–71

Nagel, Ernest, 66
Naturalism: 64, 72, 73, 74–83, 86–87, 88; Ransom as naturalist, xiv, xvi, 66–67, 68, 100; criticized by Ransom, 58; Stevens as naturalist, 85, 98; and Wordsworth, 94–95; Hardy as naturalist, 96, 97
Neurath, Otto, 68, 70
New Criticism, xiii, 106
New Realists, 43
Nietzsche, Friedrich, 11n, 81n

O'Brien, Conor Cruise, 66
O'Brien, Michael, xiv
Orthodox church, 48, 56
Oxford, University of: 3, 14, 37, 38, 40, 41, 61; and Ransom, 7–13

Pater, Walter, 42, 74
Paul, Saint, 32
Perry, R. B., 43
Pinsky, Robert, 30
Plato, 8, 12, 15, 67, 78
Platonism, 11, 42, 53, 62, 78
Positivism: 4n, 69, 82, 86, 88, 104; Ransom's sympathy with, xiii, xvi, 2, 43, 70–71, 72, 73, 75, 76, 79–80; definition of, 68; Stevens as logical positivist, 98
Pound, Ezra, 27, 65
Pragmatism: 8, 11, 12, 61, 66, 67, 87, 90, 105; Ransom on, 9, 79, 94; definition of, 68
Psychology: xiii, 73, 76n, 82, 88, 89, 94; studied by Ransom, 7, 13; criticized by Tate, 70

Quine, W. V. O., 86

Rahv, Philip, 66
Ransom, John Crowe: life, xv, xvii, 3–4, 6, 7, 13, 14, 25, 36, 37, 60–61, 65–66, 101–102; philosophical views, xv, xvi, 2–3, 7–13, 14, 15, 39–40, 42–43, 54–58, 67–71, 76–83, 85,

86–87, 89–91, 98–99, 104–105; religious views, xv, xvi, 2, 3–6, 17–24, 26–27, 28–29, 32–33, 34–35, 38–41, 43–45, 46–63, 71–75, 80, 81–82, 85, 88, 91–92, 93, 94–99, 101, 103; on poetry, 2, 15–16, 36, 42, 62–63, 68, 75, 87, 91–92; on aesthetics, 37–38, 43–44, 45, 63, 67–68, 89–90, 97–99, 100
—works: "Alienation a Century Ago," 5; "April," 23; "Armageddon," 33–35; "Art and Mr. Santayana," 66; "Art Worries the Naturalists," 81; "The Arts and the Philosophers," 67; "Beating the Naturalists with the Stick of Drama," 81; "Bells for John Whiteside's Daughter," xvi, 30, 31–32, 33; *Chills and Fever*, 34, 35, 37, 38; "A Christmas Colloquy," 22; "Classical and Romantic," 44; "The Communities of Letters," 66; "The Concrete Universal," 91; "Conrad in Twilight," 97n; "Dead Boy," 30; "Eclogue," 35; "Ego," 25–26; "Emily Dickinson: A Poet Restored," 20; "Geometry," 21–22; "Giants for Gods," 37, 44, 45; *God Without Thunder*, xiv, 38, 39, 45, 46–61, 63, 67, 71, 72, 75, 79, 89, 92, 93, 101; "The Gothic Principle in the English Literary Tradition," 37, 40, 41; "Grace," 19–21, 23, 29–30, 33; *Grace After Meat*, 33; "The Handmaidens," 26; "Humanism at Chicago," 91–92; "The Idea of a Literary Anthropologist and What He Might Say of the *Paradise Lost* of Milton," 93; "In Amicitia," 92; "The Inorganic Muses," 66, 67, 68, 76–80, 88; "The Irish, the Gaelic, the Byzantine," 80n; "Janet Waking," 30; "Master's in the Garden Again," 97n; "Mr. Russell and Mr. Schorer," 80; "Moonlight," 21; "Necrological," xvi, 28–29,33; *The New Criticism*, 69–76, 94; "The New Criticism," 82–83; "Night Voices," 26–27, 29; "Noonday Grace," 18–19; "November," 22; "On Theodore Roethke's 'In a Dark Time,'" 92; "Our Two Worthies," 32; "Persistent Explorer," 35; "The Planetary Poet," 97–99; "A Poem Nearly Anonymous," xv; *Poems About God*, xvi, 16–24, 25, 26, 31, 33, 37, 38, 39, 47; "The Poems of T. S. Eliot: A Per-